OXFORD TRAVEL GUIDE 2024

Immerse Yourself in History, Culture, and Academic Splendor in the Heart of England

ANTONIO DEREK

All rights reserved. No part of this publication may be reproduced, distributed, or transmitted in any form or by any means, including photocopying, recording, or other electronic or mechanical methods, without the prior written permission of the publisher, except in the case of brief quotations embodied in critical reviews and certain other noncommercial uses permitted by copyright law.
Copyright©(ANTONIO DEREK), (2024)

TABLE OF CONTENTS

INTRODUCTION

CHAPTER 1: A STROLL THROUGH TIME -HISTORICAL LANDMARKS

Discovering architectural marvels and iconic sites that encapsulate centuries of tradition.

CHAPTER 2: ACADEMIC OASIS - NAVIGATING THE COLLEGES

Delving into the unique academic environments, traditions, and achievements of Oxford's renowned colleges.

CHAPTER 3: CULTURAL ODYSSEY - MUSEUMS AND ART GALLERIES

Immersing yourself in the artistic and cultural treasures that Oxford proudly preserves.

CHAPTER 4: A GASTRONOMIC JOURNEY - CULINARY DELIGHTS

Savoring the flavors of Oxford, exploring both traditional and modern culinary experiences.

CHAPTER 5: HIDDEN GEMS - SECRET GARDENS AND QUIET CORNERS

Unearthing the tranquil spots and hidden gardens that provide a peaceful escape from the bustling city.

CHAPTER 6: SCHOLARLY PURSUITS - LIBRARIES AND ACADEMIC RESOURCES

Navigating the intellectual hubs and resources that make Oxford a haven for academics.

CHAPTER 7: TRADITIONS ALIVE - FESTIVALS AND CELEBRATIONS

Participating in the vibrant festivals and cultural

celebrations that breathe life into Oxford's traditions.

CHAPTER 8: INNOVATIONS UNLEASHED - OXFORD'S TECHNOLOGICAL ADVANCEMENTS

Exploring the cutting-edge developments and technological innovations emerging from Oxford's academic sphere.

CONCLUSION

INTRODUCTION

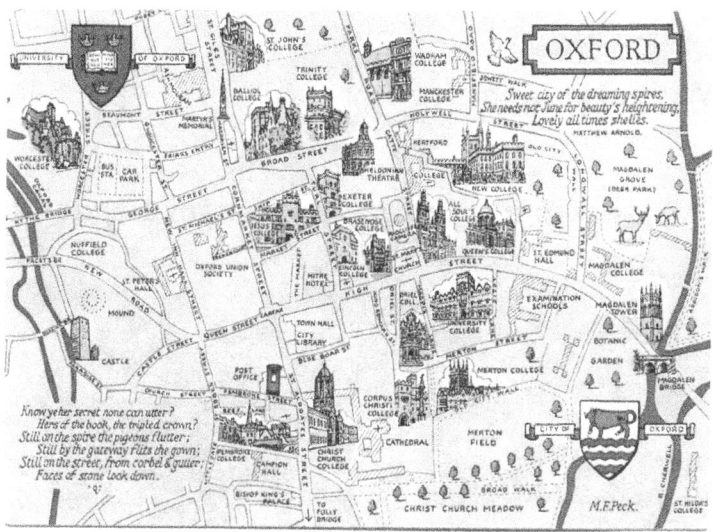

Oxford, nestled in the heart of England, boasts a rich history dating back centuries. To truly appreciate its cultural tapestry, start your exploration at the Ashmolean Museum, the world's first university museum. Founded in 1683, this cultural gem houses a diverse collection of art and artifacts. Open from 10 am to 5 pm, the Ashmolean offers a glimpse into Oxford's storied past.

Address: Beaumont St, Oxford OX1 2PH, United Kingdom

Contact: +44 1865 278000

Website: Ashmolean Museum

Discovering Oxford's Literary Legacy

No journey through Oxford is complete without delving into its literary legacy. Head to the Bodleian Library, a haven for book lovers. Established in

1602, the Bodleian is not only a repository of knowledge but also an architectural marvel. Take a guided tour, available from 9:30 am to 5 pm, to explore hidden gems within its historic walls.

Address: Broad St, Oxford OX1 3BG, United Kingdom
Contact: +44 1865 277162
Website: Bodleian Library

Strolling Through Oxford's Quaint Streets

Immerse yourself in Oxford's charm by taking a leisurely stroll through the cobbled streets of the city center. The Covered Market, open from 8 am to 5:30 pm, is a perfect starting point. Indulge in a shopping experience that spans from traditional English sweets to handmade crafts, capturing the essence of Oxford's local culture.

Address: Market St, Oxford OX1 3DZ, United Kingdom

Dining Amidst Oxford's Elegance

As the day unfolds, treat yourself to the culinary delights that Oxford has to offer. The Ivy Oxford Brasserie, located at 120-121 High St, boasts an elegant atmosphere and a menu that fuses modern British dishes with international flavors. Open from 8 am to 11 pm, it provides a perfect setting to savor a delightful meal.

Address: 120-121 High St, Oxford OX1 4DF, United Kingdom
Contact: +44 1865 248695
Website: The Ivy Oxford Brasserie

Reveling in Oxford's Nightlife

As the sun sets, Oxford's nightlife comes to life. The Turf Tavern, a historic pub tucked away in Bath Pl, is a local favorite. With its cozy ambiance and a selection of fine ales, it's an ideal spot to unwind. Open until 11 pm, this pub encapsulates the convivial spirit of Oxford after dark.

Address: 4-5 Bath Pl, Oxford OX1 3SU, United Kingdom
Contact: +44 1865 243235

Budget-Friendly Exploration

For those seeking a more economical adventure, Oxford offers a variety of free walking tours. Oxford Walking Tours provides informative and entertaining guides who lead you through the city's nooks and crannies. Don't forget to tip your guide, and you'll find this experience both enlightening and affordable.

Website: Oxford Walking Tours

In conclusion, Oxford's rich history and vibrant culture are waiting to be unveiled. Whether you immerse yourself in the treasures of the Ashmolean Museum, explore the literary wonders of the Bodleian Library, stroll through the charming streets, indulge in culinary delights at The Ivy Oxford Brasserie, or embrace the nightlife at The Turf Tavern, each experience contributes to the tapestry of Oxford's allure. Whether you have a penchant for history, literature, or simply savoring the local atmosphere, Oxford has something to offer every discerning traveler. So, step into this cultural haven and let the magic of Oxford captivate your senses.

Experiencing Oxford's Academic Prestige

No exploration of Oxford is complete without delving into its academic prestige. Take a guided tour of the University of Oxford, where the likes of J.R.R. Tolkien and Oscar Wilde once roamed. The tour includes iconic landmarks such as the Radcliffe Camera and the Bridge of Sighs. Tours run daily from 10 am to 4:30 pm, providing a captivating glimpse into the intellectual legacy of this esteemed institution.

Address: University Offices, Wellington Square, Oxford OX1 2JD, United Kingdom
Contact: +44 1865 270000
Website: University of Oxford

Punting on the Cherwell River

For a leisurely afternoon, experience the timeless tradition of punting on the Cherwell River. Head to Magdalen Bridge Boathouse, where you can rent a punt and glide along the serene waters. The boathouse is open from 9 am to 5 pm, offering a picturesque escape from the bustling city. Punting fees typically range from $25 to $40 per hour, depending on the boat size and duration.

Address: 1-2 Magdalen Bridge, Oxford OX1 4AU, United Kingdom
Contact: +44 1865 202643
Website: Magdalen Bridge Boathouse

Embracing the Botanical Beauty

Nature enthusiasts will find solace in the Oxford Botanic Garden, founded in 1621. This oasis of greenery showcases a diverse collection of plants and flowers. Open from 9 am to 6 pm, it's an ideal spot for a leisurely stroll or a contemplative moment amidst nature's beauty.

Address: Rose Ln, Oxford OX1 4AZ, United Kingdom

Contact: +44 1865 286690

Website: Oxford Botanic Garden

Accommodation: A Restful Reprieve

Ensure your stay in Oxford is as comfortable as it is immersive by choosing the right accommodation. The Randolph Hotel, located in the heart of the city, offers a blend of luxury and history. With its charming Victorian architecture and modern amenities, it's a perfect base for your exploration. Room rates typically start from $200 per night.

Address: Beaumont St, Oxford OX1 2LN, United Kingdom

Contact: +44 1865 256400

Website: The Randolph Hotel

Practical Tips for Maximum Enjoyment

Timing Matters: Plan your visits during weekdays to avoid crowds, especially at popular attractions like the Ashmolean Museum and Bodleian Library.

Guided Tours: Invest in guided tours for a more enriching experience. Knowledgeable guides bring history to life and provide insights you might otherwise miss.

Dine Off-Peak: To fully relish your dining experience, consider dining slightly earlier or later than peak hours. This not only ensures a more intimate setting but also allows you to savor the culinary delights without rushing.

Punting Reservations: If you plan to punt on the Cherwell River, consider making reservations in advance, especially during weekends and peak tourist seasons.

Accommodation Booking: Secure your accommodation well in advance, especially if you plan to visit during Oxford's busy events or graduation periods.

In essence, to make the most of your Oxford adventure, immerse yourself in its academic prestige, relax with a punt on the Cherwell River, embrace the botanical beauty of the Oxford Botanic Garden, and ensure a restful reprieve at the Randolph Hotel. By incorporating these experiences and practical tips, you're set to unravel the layers of Oxford's allure, creating memories that linger long after your journey through this captivating city.

CHAPTER 1: A STROLL THROUGH TIME - HISTORICAL LANDMARKS

Discovering architectural marvels and iconic sites that encapsulate centuries of tradition.

Opening with a sense of intrigue and allure, let's embark on a captivating journey through Oxford's historical landmarks, where centuries-old tales are etched into the very stones beneath your feet.

Oxford Castle and Prison: Unraveling Centuries of Stories

Location: Oxford OX1 1AY, United Kingdom
Contact: +44 1865 260666

Website: Oxford Castle and Prison

Hours: 10:00 AM – 4:20 PM (Monday-Sunday)

As you step into the grandeur of Oxford Castle, let the echoes of the past guide you through its ancient corridors. Immerse yourself in a guided tour for an intimate exploration of the prison's dark history, complete with tales of notorious inmates and the evolution of justice over the centuries. Average cost: $20.

Bodleian Library: A Literary Haven Frozen in Time

Location: Broad St, Oxford OX1 3BG, United Kingdom

Contact: +44 1865 277162

Website: Bodleian Library

Hours: 9:00 AM – 5:00 PM (Monday-Saturday)

Delve into the world of academia at the Bodleian Library, a haven for literary enthusiasts. Take a guided tour to witness the architectural splendor of Duke Humfrey's Library, dating back to the 15th century, and marvel at priceless manuscripts. Average cost: $15.

University Church of St. Mary the Virgin: A Pinnacle of Ecclesiastical Elegance

Location: High St, Oxford OX1 4BJ, United Kingdom
Contact: +44 1865 279111
Website: St. Mary's Church
Hours: 9:00 AM – 5:00 PM (Monday-Saturday), 11:30 AM – 5:00 PM (Sunday)

Ascend the tower of St. Mary's Church for a breathtaking panorama of Oxford's skyline. This architectural gem, with roots dating back to the 13th century, invites you to attend evensong or explore its rich history during daylight hours. Average cost: $8.

Christ Church College: A Majestic Blend of Academia and History

Location: St Aldates, Oxford OX1 1DP, United Kingdom
Contact: +44 1865 276492
Website: Christ Church College
Hours: 10:00 AM – 5:00 PM (Monday-Sunday)

Wander through the hallowed halls of Christ Church College, a living testament to Oxford's academic legacy. Opt for a guided tour to unearth the secrets of the Great Hall, famously featured in the Harry Potter films, and explore the serene meadows surrounding the college. Average cost: $18.

Ashmolean Museum: Art and Antiquities Preserved in Splendor

Location: Beaumont St, Oxford OX1 2PH, United Kingdom

Contact: +44 1865 278000

Website: Ashmolean Museum

Hours: 10:00 AM – 5:00 PM (Tuesday-Sunday)

Immerse yourself in the cultural tapestry of Oxford at the Ashmolean Museum. With artifacts spanning millennia, this museum offers a captivating journey through art and antiquities. Join a thematic tour to gain deeper insights into the museum's extensive collection. Average cost: $12.

As you traverse these historical landmarks, consider investing in an Oxford Pass for a comprehensive experience. Priced at $50, this pass grants access to all mentioned attractions, saving you up to 20% on individual tickets. Ensure to check the official websites for any updated information on opening hours and special events. Oxford's history awaits, inviting you to become a part of its timeless narrative.

Radcliffe Camera: Oxford's Pantheon of Knowledge

Location: Radcliffe Square, Oxford OX1 4AJ, United Kingdom

Contact: +44 1865 277162

Website: Radcliffe Camera

Hours: Exterior views available at all times, Interior tours 9:30 AM – 5:00 PM (Monday-Saturday)

Marvel at the iconic Radcliffe Camera, a neoclassical masterpiece housing some of Oxford's finest collections. While the exterior can be admired at any time, guided interior tours reveal the secrets within, showcasing the history of this architectural gem. Average cost: $10.

Bridge of Sighs: A Picturesque Passage through Time

Location: New College Ln, Oxford OX1 3BL, United Kingdom

Meander along New College Lane to encounter the whimsical Bridge of Sighs, reminiscent of its Venetian namesake. Built in 1914, this charming bridge connects two parts of Hertford College. Capture the essence of Oxford's architectural charm and make sure to visit during daylight hours for optimal photo opportunities.

Carfax Tower: Panoramic Views of Oxford's Skyline

Location: Queen St, Oxford OX1 1ET, United Kingdom

Contact: +44 1865 236251

Website: Carfax Tower

Hours: 10:00 AM – 5:00 PM (Monday-Sunday)

Ascend the Carfax Tower for an unparalleled view of Oxford's skyline. Dating back to the 12th century, this tower stands as a historic landmark in the heart of the city. Enjoy breathtaking views of the dreaming spires and beyond. Average cost: $5.

Oxford Botanic Garden: A Tranquil Oasis in the Heart of the City

Location: Rose Ln, Oxford OX1 4AZ, United Kingdom

Contact: +44 1865 286690

Website: Botanic Garden

Hours: 9:00 AM – 4:00 PM (Monday-Sunday)

Take a leisurely stroll through the Oxford Botanic Garden, a serene haven dating back to 1621. Admire the diverse plant collections, themed borders, and the peaceful atmosphere. Guided tours are available, providing in-depth insights into the botanical wonders within. Average cost: $7.

A comprehensive exploration of Oxford's historical landmarks promises an enriching experience. Consider a combined ticket for Radcliffe Camera, Carfax Tower, and Bridge of Sighs, priced at $20, to maximize your cultural immersion. Remember to embrace the timeless beauty of Oxford by taking leisurely strolls between these landmarks, allowing the city's history to unfold before your eyes. Capture moments, savor the architecture, and let the essence of centuries past seep into your soul as you embark on this unforgettable journey through time in Oxford.

Location: Port Meadow, Oxford OX2 0NJ, United Kingdom

Escape the urban bustle and venture to the untamed beauty of Port Meadow. Stretching along the River Thames, this expansive meadow offers a tranquil retreat with a history dating back to prehistoric times. Take a leisurely walk or enjoy a picnic while absorbing the panoramic views of Oxford's spires. Accessible at all times, this natural gem provides a perfect contrast to the city's historical architecture.

Museum of the History of Science: Unveiling Oxford's Scientific Legacy

Location: Broad St, Oxford OX1 3AZ, United Kingdom

Contact: +44 1865 277280

Website: Museum of the History of Science

Hours: 12:00 PM – 5:00 PM (Tuesday-Sunday)

Engage with Oxford's scientific heritage at the Museum of the History of Science. Housed in the world's oldest surviving purpose-built museum building, this institution showcases instruments that have shaped scientific understanding. Explore the evolution of scientific thought through interactive exhibits. Average cost: $10.

Oxford Covered Market: A Gastronomic and Artistic Haven

Location: Market St, Oxford OX1 3DZ, United Kingdom

Contact: +44 1865 242823

Website: Covered Market

Hours: 8:00 AM – 5:30 PM (Monday-Saturday), 10:00 AM – 4:00 PM (Sunday)

Immerse yourself in the lively atmosphere of Oxford Covered Market, a historic market dating back to the 18th century. Indulge in diverse culinary delights, from artisanal chocolates to international cuisine. Unearth unique artworks, crafts, and clothing, creating a perfect blend of tradition and modernity. No entrance fee; prices vary based on purchases.

Pitt Rivers Museum: A Global Tapestry of Cultures

Location: South Parks Rd, Oxford OX1 3PP, United Kingdom

Contact: +44 1865 270927

Website: Pitt Rivers Museum

Hours: 10:00 AM – 4:30 PM (Tuesday-Sunday)

Explore the anthropological wonders at the Pitt Rivers Museum, known for its eclectic collection spanning cultures worldwide. Admire artifacts from diverse societies and civilizations, each with its unique narrative. Engage in guided tours for a deeper understanding of the museum's ethnographic treasures. Average cost: $12.

As you delve into these additional facets of Oxford's cultural and natural tapestry, remember that the city's charm lies not only in its historical landmarks but also in the harmonious blend of tradition, innovation, and nature. Capture the essence of each location, savor the flavors of the covered market, and let the stories from Pitt Rivers Museum resonate within you. Oxford's timeless allure extends beyond architectural marvels, inviting you to experience the full spectrum of its rich heritage.

CHAPTER 2: ACADEMIC OASIS - NAVIGATING THE COLLEGES

Delving into the unique academic environments, traditions, and achievements of Oxford's renowned colleges.

Embark on a scholarly journey through the hallowed halls of Oxford's prestigious colleges, where history, tradition, and academic excellence converge. This guide will illuminate the distinct academic environments and achievements that make each college a microcosm of intellectual richness.

Christ Church College: A Tapestry of History and Learning

Nestled in St Aldates, Oxford, Christ Church College stands as a beacon of historical significance and academic prowess. Explore the grandeur of the Great Hall, reminiscent of Hogwarts, where scenes from the Harry Potter films were shot. Immerse yourself in the architectural marvel of Tom Quad, a masterpiece dating back to the 16th century.

Entry Fee: $15

Opening Hours: 10:00 AM - 5:00 PM (Monday-Saturday), 2:00 PM - 5:00 PM (Sunday)

Magdalen College: Serenity by the Cherwell

Magdalen College, situated along the picturesque banks of the River Cherwell, offers a serene academic escape. Stroll through the Magdalen Deer Park, where the rustle of leaves accompanies your contemplative thoughts. Ascend to the top of Magdalen Tower for panoramic views of the dreaming spires.

Entry Fee: $10

Opening Hours: 9:00 AM - 6:00 PM (Daily)

Balliol College: Intellectual Haven

A haven for intellectuals, Balliol College has nurtured some of the world's brightest minds. Engage in the vibrant academic atmosphere by attending public lectures and discussions. The college library is a treasure trove of knowledge, allowing visitors to delve into its extensive collection.

Entry Fee: $8

Opening Hours: 9:30 AM - 4:30 PM (Monday-Saturday), Closed on Sunday

Trinity College: Courtyards and Gardens of Learning

Trinity College beckons with its splendid courtyards and meticulously landscaped gardens. Take a leisurely stroll through the Fellows' Garden, an oasis of tranquility amid the academic rigors. Don't miss the Wren Library, a masterpiece by Sir Christopher Wren, housing rare manuscripts.

Entry Fee: $12

Opening Hours: 10:00 AM - 5:00 PM (Monday-Saturday), 12:30 PM - 2:30 PM (Sunday)

St John's College: Where Tradition Meets Modernity

St John's College seamlessly blends tradition with modernity. Explore the Bridge of Sighs, an iconic Oxford landmark, and witness the contrast of historical architecture with the contemporary St John's College Auditorium, hosting cutting-edge academic events.

Entry Fee: $10

Opening Hours: 9:00 AM - 5:00 PM (Daily)

Tips for Getting the Most Out of Your Visit:

Purchase a combined ticket for multiple colleges to save on entry fees. Many colleges offer bundled tickets at a discounted rate.

Check the academic calendar for each college to coincide your visit with events like lectures, seminars, or cultural festivals.

Utilize guided tours provided by the colleges or hire a local guide well-versed in Oxford's academic history. The additional insights can enhance your understanding of the colleges' significance.

Closing:

Intricately woven into the fabric of Oxford's academic landscape, these colleges are more than mere institutions; they are living chronicles of intellectual evolution. Embrace the opportunity to immerse yourself in the traditions, achievements, and architectural wonders that define Oxford's academic oasis.

Keble College: Neo-Gothic Splendor

Keble College's neo-Gothic architecture is a visual feast for enthusiasts of intricate design. Admire the stunning Keble Chapel, known for its mesmerizing stained glass windows. Take a moment in the college's peaceful quad, surrounded by the harmony of Victorian aesthetics.

Entry Fee: $10
Opening Hours: 10:30 AM - 4:30 PM (Monday-Saturday), 1:00 PM - 4:30 PM (Sunday)
Pembroke College: Literary Legacy

Pembroke College boasts a rich literary legacy, with alumni including the likes of J.R.R. Tolkien. Wander through the college's serene gardens and explore the Founders' Library, where rare manuscripts and first editions are housed. The ambiance here is a testament to the college's commitment to the written word.

Entry Fee: $8

Opening Hours: 9:00 AM - 5:00 PM (Monday-Saturday), Closed on Sunday

Wadham College: Artistic Haven

Wadham College is a haven for art enthusiasts, with an impressive collection of modern and contemporary art. The Clore Old Library hosts rotating exhibitions, showcasing the intersection of art and academia. The college's gardens provide a peaceful retreat for contemplation.

Entry Fee: $12

Opening Hours: 10:00 AM - 4:00 PM (Monday-Saturday), 1:00 PM - 4:00 PM (Sunday)

Brasenose College: Timeless Elegance

Brasenose College exudes timeless elegance with its historic quad and the imposing Radcliffe Camera nearby. Visit the college chapel, adorned with exquisite woodwork and stained glass. The Old Quad, dating back to the 17th century, is a prime example of architectural grace.

Entry Fee: $10

Opening Hours: 9:30 AM - 5:00 PM (Monday-Saturday), Closed on Sunday

Maximizing Your Experience:

Engage with the college community by attending open lectures or participating in public events. Many colleges offer opportunities for visitors to interact with students and professors.

Don't rush your visit. Allocate sufficient time to explore each college thoroughly, allowing for spontaneous discoveries and absorbing the unique atmosphere of each institution.

Consider purchasing a city-wide pass that includes access to multiple attractions, including Oxford's colleges. This can offer substantial savings for avid explorers.

Conclusion: A Tapestry of Knowledge Unveiled

Oxford's colleges are more than landmarks; they are living embodiments of intellectual pursuit and academic excellence. As you navigate through these academic oases, each one unfolds a unique chapter in the story of human knowledge. Embrace the opportunity to connect with centuries of learning, and let the echoes of scholarly endeavors resonate as you wander through the time-honored halls of Oxford's distinguished colleges.

Wolfson College: Modernity in Academia

Wolfson College stands as a testament to Oxford's commitment to modernity. The modern architecture of the Wolfson Academic Building complements the traditional surroundings, offering a glimpse into Oxford's forward-thinking approach. Explore the Jacqueline Du Pré Music Building, a contemporary masterpiece hosting a variety of cultural events.

Entry Fee: $10

Opening Hours: 9:00 AM - 6:00 PM (Monday-Friday), Closed on Weekends

Lincoln College: Hidden Gem

Lincoln College, often considered a hidden gem, welcomes visitors with its charming medieval library and serene garden. The intimacy of this college provides a more personal connection to Oxford's academic legacy. Attend a choir rehearsal in the chapel for a melodic experience in this quiet retreat.

Entry Fee: $8

Opening Hours: 10:30 AM - 4:30 PM (Monday-Saturday), 1:30 PM - 4:30 PM (Sunday)

Oriel College: Architectural Elegance

Oriel College boasts architectural elegance with its beautiful Tudor-style frontage. Admire the college's iconic statue of the Provost, Cardinal Newman, and explore the Hall and Chapel, showcasing intricate detailing. The quad's timeless beauty is enhanced by the Provost's Garden, a peaceful sanctuary.

Entry Fee: $12

Opening Hours: 10:00 AM - 5:00 PM (Monday-Saturday), 2:00 PM - 5:00 PM (Sunday)

St Hilda's College: Feminine Grace in Academia

St Hilda's College, originally a women-only college, radiates feminine grace and intellectual prowess. Explore the serene gardens and attend events that celebrate the achievements of women in academia. The college offers a unique perspective on the evolving landscape of Oxford's academic history.

Entry Fee: $10

Opening Hours: 9:30 AM - 4:30 PM (Monday-Saturday), 1:30 PM - 4:30 PM (Sunday)

Making the Most of Your Academic Journey:

Engage with college life by dining at college halls or cafeterias, experiencing the daily routines of students.

Plan your visit during term time to witness the vibrant energy of academic life, with students hustling between classes and engaging in intellectual discussions.

Connect with college alumni networks to gain insights into the contemporary academic and social landscape of each institution.

Navigating the colleges of Oxford is not just a visual spectacle; it's an immersive experience into the rich tapestry of academic diversity. From medieval libraries to modern architectural wonders, each college contributes a unique note to the symphony of knowledge. As you traverse the cobblestone streets and traverse the quads, remember that you are not just a visitor; you are partaking in a timeless academic journey, surrounded by the echoes of centuries of learning.

CHAPTER 3: CULTURAL ODYSSEY - MUSEUMS AND ART GALLERIES

Immersing yourself in the artistic and cultural treasures that Oxford proudly preserves.

Embark on a Cultural Odyssey in Oxford, where the city's rich history and vibrant art scene come together in an enchanting tapestry of museums and art galleries. Here's a guide to help you navigate this cultural haven and make the most of your experience:

Ashmolean Museum: A Timeless Treasure Trove

Address: Beaumont Street, Oxford, OX1 2PH, United Kingdom

Contact: +44 1865 278000

Opening Hours: 10:00 AM - 5:00 PM (Closed on Mondays)

Admission Fee: $15 for adults, $8 for students

The Ashmolean Museum, the world's first university museum, houses an extensive collection spanning art and archaeology. Dive into millennia of human history, from ancient civilizations to contemporary art. To maximize your visit, consider joining one of their guided tours, offered daily at 2:00 PM. The insight provided by knowledgeable guides adds depth to your exploration.

Pitt Rivers Museum: Unveiling Anthropological Wonders

Address: South Parks Road, Oxford, OX1 3PP, United Kingdom

Contact: +44 1865 270927

Opening Hours: 10:00 AM - 4:30 PM (Closed on Mondays)

Admission Fee: Free, but donations are encouraged

Step into the Pitt Rivers Museum, a treasure trove of anthropological artifacts and curiosities. The dimly lit ambiance adds a mystique to your journey through diverse cultures. Engage fully by attending one of their themed evening events, such as "Magic and Rituals," where the museum comes alive with performances and talks. Don't forget to make a donation to support their commitment to free admission.

Modern Art Oxford: Where Innovation Meets Aesthetics

Address: 30 Pembroke Street, Oxford, OX1 1BP, United Kingdom

Contact: +44 1865 722733

Opening Hours: 11:00 AM - 6:00 PM (Closed on Mondays)

Admission Fee: $10 for adults, $5 for students (Free entry for under 18s)

Immerse yourself in contemporary art at Modern Art Oxford, a hub of innovation and artistic expression. Enhance your experience by participating in one of their art workshops or artist-led talks, providing valuable insights into the creative process. Check their website for upcoming events, and plan your visit accordingly to coincide with exhibitions that align with your artistic preferences.

Museum of the History of Science: Bridging Past and Present

Address: Broad Street, Oxford, OX1 3AZ, United Kingdom

Contact: +44 1865 277280

Opening Hours: 12:00 PM - 5:00 PM (Closed on Mondays)

Admission Fee: $12 for adults, $6 for students

Uncover the evolution of scientific thought at the Museum of the History of Science. Attend their daily object handling sessions at 2:00 PM, where you can interact with historical scientific instruments. This hands-on experience provides a unique perspective on the scientific advancements that have shaped our world. Take advantage of their guided tours to delve deeper into the stories behind the exhibits.

Oxford University Press Museum: Celebrating Literary Legacy

Address: Great Clarendon Street, Oxford, OX2 6DP, United Kingdom

Contact: +44 1865 353979

Opening Hours: 10:00 AM - 4:00 PM (Closed on weekends)

Admission Fee: Free

Explore the birthplace of countless literary masterpieces at the Oxford University Press Museum. Delve into the history of printing and publishing, showcasing the evolution of written communication. Enhance your visit by attending one of their scheduled talks, shedding light on the intricate process of bringing words to print. As admission is free, consider making a contribution to support the museum's preservation efforts.

Oxford's museums and art galleries offer a kaleidoscope of cultural experiences. To fully immerse yourself, plan your visits strategically, taking advantage of guided tours, thematic events, and interactive sessions. Remember, each admission fee contributes to the preservation and continued enrichment of these cultural institutions, ensuring that future generations can also embark on their own Cultural Odyssey in this historical city.

When you embark on your cultural odyssey through Oxford, take a moment to revel in the city's architectural splendor. The journey between these cultural gems becomes an exploration of cobblestone streets, picturesque gardens, and centuries-old buildings, enriching your experience beyond the confines of the museums and art galleries.

As you stroll from the Ashmolean Museum to the Pitt Rivers Museum, pause at the Radcliffe Camera, an iconic neoclassical building that serves as a symbol of Oxford's intellectual prowess. Capture the moment, surrounded by the harmonious blend of history and academia. The nearby University Church of St. Mary the Virgin offers breathtaking views of the city from its tower, providing a serene interlude in your cultural expedition.

Modern Art Oxford beckons with its contemporary allure, nestled amid the charming streets of Pembroke. Venture into the Covered Market nearby for a taste of Oxford's culinary delights. The market, a historic shopping destination since the 18th century, boasts diverse stalls, from artisanal chocolatiers to traditional English butchers. Savor local flavors and recharge before delving into the vibrant world of modern art.

The Museum of the History of Science, located on Broad Street, invites you to explore the intersection of science and society. Before or after your visit, explore the historic Bodleian Library, one of the oldest libraries in Europe. Join a guided tour to wander through the Divinity School, the Convocation House, and the Duke Humfrey's Library, each a testament to Oxford's commitment to knowledge.

Conclude your cultural journey at the Oxford University Press Museum, tucked away on Great Clarendon Street. After immersing yourself in the world of literature and publishing, meander through the University Parks, a sprawling expanse of greenery along the Cherwell River. Unwind by the water, perhaps with a book you picked up from one of Oxford's quaint bookshops, continuing the narrative of your cultural exploration.

Remember to check the respective museum and gallery websites for any temporary exhibitions or special events that might coincide with your visit. Many institutions offer memberships or special packages, providing an economical way for avid culture enthusiasts to make the most of their time in Oxford.

In the evenings, explore Oxford's culinary scene and enjoy a meal at one of the city's charming restaurants. The combination of delectable cuisine and the intellectual ambiance lingering from the day's cultural immersion creates a perfect symphony for the senses.

Let this cultural odyssey through Oxford be more than a checklist of museums; let it be a narrative woven through the city's streets, historical landmarks, and contemporary spaces. Immerse yourself not only in the art on display but in the atmosphere that makes Oxford a haven for culture connoisseurs.

Extend your Cultural Odyssey by venturing into Oxford's vibrant arts community beyond the traditional museum spaces. Explore local galleries and exhibitions that showcase the talents of emerging artists, adding a dynamic layer to your cultural experience.

OVADA - Oxford Visual Arts Development Agency: Nurturing Creativity

Address: 14A Osney Lane, Oxford, OX1 1NJ, United Kingdom

Contact: +44 1865 200951

Opening Hours: Vary (Check website for current exhibitions)

Delve into the contemporary art scene at OVADA, an artist-led space supporting the development of visual arts in Oxford. Admission is often free, and the ever-changing exhibitions feature a diverse array of mediums, from paintings to installations. Attend one of their artist talks or workshops to engage directly with the local art community and gain insight into the creative process.

The Jam Factory: Fusion of Art and Dining

Address: 27 Park End Street, Oxford, OX1 1HU, United Kingdom
Contact: +44 1865 244613
Opening Hours: 8:00 AM - 11:00 PM (Closed on Mondays)

Indulge in a sensory experience at The Jam Factory, a unique venue that seamlessly integrates art, food, and community. Admire the contemporary art exhibitions adorning the walls while enjoying a meal crafted from locally sourced ingredients. The space also hosts regular art events and live music, adding an eclectic touch to your cultural exploration.

Oxford Printmakers Cooperative: Celebrating Printmaking Craftsmanship

Address: 1st Floor, Tyndale House, 26-29 Beaumont Street, Oxford, OX1 2NP, United Kingdom

Contact: +44 1865 512221

Opening Hours: Vary (Check website for current exhibitions)

Discover the art of printmaking at the Oxford Printmakers Cooperative. This cooperative space showcases the work of local printmakers, and you might even find unique pieces available for purchase. Consider attending one of their printmaking workshops to try your hand at this traditional craft and gain a deeper appreciation for the art form.

The North Wall Arts Centre: Where Performance Meets Visual Arts

Address: South Parade, Oxford, OX2 7JN, United Kingdom

Contact: +44 1865 319450

Opening Hours: Vary (Check website for current exhibitions)

This multifaceted arts center combines visual arts with live performances. Explore the gallery spaces featuring contemporary artwork, and then catch a play, dance performance, or live music event in the adjoining theater. The North Wall Arts Centre fosters a dynamic cultural environment, providing a holistic experience for art enthusiasts.

As you extend your cultural journey into these additional spaces, keep an eye on local events calendars for art fairs, street performances, or pop-up exhibitions that might coincide with your visit. Oxford's arts scene is not confined to designated spaces; it spills into the streets, creating an immersive atmosphere for those eager to explore beyond the conventional.

In the evenings, wind down at one of Oxford's historic pubs, where the ambiance is steeped in centuries of literary and artistic conversations. Engage with locals, share your experiences, and absorb the creative energy that permeates this timeless city. Let your Cultural Odyssey be a tapestry woven not only with the threads of historical artifacts but also with the vibrant hues of contemporary and local artistry.

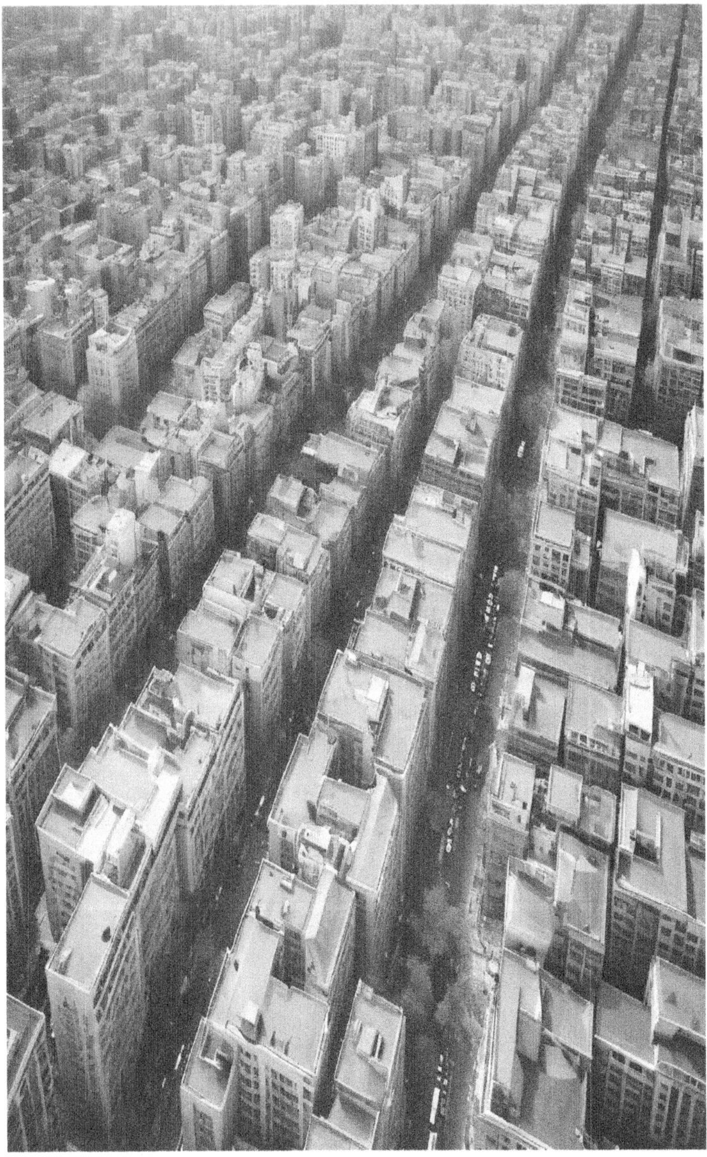

CHAPTER 4: A GASTRONOMIC JOURNEY - CULINARY DELIGHTS

Savoring the flavors of Oxford, exploring both traditional and modern culinary experiences.

Embark on a delectable journey through the gastronomic wonders of Oxford, where the fusion of traditional and contemporary flavors creates a culinary tapestry that captivates the senses.

Here's your guide to savoring the best of Oxford's culinary delights:

Start Your Day with a Hearty Breakfast at The Nosebag:

Address: 6-8 St Michael's St, Oxford OX1 2DU, United Kingdom

Opening Hours: 8:00 AM - 11:30 AM (Monday to Sunday)

Contact: +44 1865 721033

Indulge in a quintessential English breakfast at The Nosebag, an iconic eatery nestled in the heart of Oxford. From the perfectly poached eggs to the locally sourced sausages, this establishment sets the tone for a day filled with culinary bliss. The average cost for a satisfying breakfast experience is around $12 per person.

Explore the Covered Market for Local Delicacies:

Address: Market St, Oxford OX1 3DZ, United Kingdom

Opening Hours: 8:00 AM - 5:30 PM (Monday to Saturday), 10:00 AM - 4:00 PM (Sunday)

Immerse yourself in the vibrant atmosphere of Oxford's Covered Market, a treasure trove of local delicacies and artisanal treats. From fresh produce to handmade chocolates, the market caters to every palate. Sample a variety of cheeses at the Oxford Cheese Company or savor the delectable pastries at Ben's Cookies. Allocate around $20 for a delightful market experience.

Lunch at The Trout Inn by the River Thames:

Address: 195 Godstow Rd, Wolvercote, Oxford OX2 8PN, United Kingdom

Opening Hours: 12:00 PM - 3:00 PM (Monday to Sunday)

Contact: +44 1865 510930

Enjoy a picturesque riverside lunch at The Trout Inn, situated along the tranquil River Thames. Relish their renowned fish and chips or opt for a gourmet burger paired with a local ale. With an average cost of $25 per person, this culinary gem offers a blend of exquisite flavors and a charming ambiance.

Afternoon Tea at The Grand Cafe:

Address: 84 High St, Oxford OX1 4BG, United Kingdom
Opening Hours: 8:00 AM - 11:00 PM (Monday to Sunday)
Contact: +44 1865 204463

Treat yourself to an indulgent afternoon tea at The Grand Cafe, the oldest coffeehouse in England. Sip on premium teas accompanied by an array of delicate pastries and sandwiches. The sophisticated setting and impeccable service elevate the experience. Expect to spend around $30 per person for this quintessentially British affair.

Fine Dining at Brasserie Blanc:

Address: 71-72 Walton St, Oxford OX2 6AG, United Kingdom
Opening Hours: 12:00 PM - 10:00 PM (Monday to Sunday)
Contact: +44 1865 510999

Conclude your culinary journey with an exquisite dinner at Brasserie Blanc, a renowned French restaurant in Oxford. Chef Raymond Blanc's culinary prowess shines through in dishes like Coq au Vin and Tarte Tatin. The average cost for a three-course dinner is approximately $50 per person, providing a taste of refined French cuisine in the heart of Oxford.

Culinary Workshops at The Foodie School:

Address: 45 Iffley Rd, Oxford OX4 1EA, United Kingdom

Contact: +44 1865 595313

Enhance your culinary skills with hands-on workshops at The Foodie School. Learn the art of crafting pasta from scratch or master the nuances of wine pairing. Prices vary based on the selected workshop, ranging from $30 to $80 per session. Check their website for workshop schedules and unleash your inner chef.

Maximize your gastronomic adventure by embracing the diverse culinary landscape Oxford has to offer. From traditional markets to riverside inns and fine dining establishments, each experience contributes to a harmonious blend of flavors that define the city's culinary identity.

Unwind with a Nightcap at The Varsity Club Rooftop Bar:

Address: 9 High St, Oxford OX1 4DB, United Kingdom

Opening Hours: 12:00 PM - 1:00 AM (Monday to Sunday)

Contact: +44 1865 248777

Conclude your culinary odyssey with a breathtaking view of Oxford from The Varsity Club's Rooftop Bar. Sip on expertly crafted cocktails while soaking in the city lights. The ambiance and the extensive drink menu make it a perfect spot for a nightcap. Budget around $15 for a delightful end to your gastronomic journey.

Participate in a Tasting Tour with Oxford Foodie Tours:

Address: Meeting point varies, check website for details

Contact: info@oxfordfoodietours.com

For a comprehensive exploration of Oxford's culinary scene, consider joining a tasting tour with Oxford Foodie Tours. These guided tours take you to hidden gems, offering insights into the city's food culture. Prices start at $40 per person, and reservations can be made through their website. Tours typically last 2-3 hours, providing a delightful mix of history and gastronomy.

Culinary Events at Oxford Food & Drink Festival:

Address: Various locations, check festival schedule

Website: Oxford Food & Drink Festival

Plan your visit to coincide with the Oxford Food & Drink Festival, an annual celebration of local and international cuisines. The festival showcases food markets, cooking demonstrations, and tasting events. Entry fees vary, but the culinary experiences are worth the investment. Check the festival website for details on upcoming events, participating vendors, and ticket prices.

Experience Molecular Gastronomy at The Oxford Kitchen:

Address: 215 Banbury Rd, Oxford OX2 7HQ, United Kingdom

Opening Hours: 12:00 PM - 2:30 PM, 6:30 PM - 9:30 PM (Tuesday to Saturday), 12:00 PM - 4:00 PM (Sunday)

Contact: +44 1865 511149

Elevate your culinary adventure with a visit to The Oxford Kitchen, where modern techniques meet traditional flavors. Indulge in dishes crafted using molecular gastronomy, showcasing the artistry of the culinary team. The tasting menu, priced at $80 per person, promises an avant-garde dining experience that pushes the boundaries of taste and presentation.

Savoring Oxford's culinary delights extends beyond individual meals; it encompasses a rich tapestry of experiences. From rooftop bars to tasting tours and festivals, the city's gastronomic offerings cater to every palate. Embrace the diversity, immerse yourself in culinary workshops, and leave Oxford with not just a satisfied appetite but a deep appreciation for its vibrant and evolving food culture.

Unique Dessert Experience at G&D's Ice Cream:

Address: 55 Little Clarendon St, Oxford OX1 2HS, United Kingdom

Opening Hours: 12:00 PM - 11:00 PM (Monday to Sunday)

Contact: +44 1865 516652

Indulge your sweet tooth at G&D's Ice Cream, a beloved local spot known for its creative and extensive ice cream flavors. From classic vanilla to adventurous combinations like Honeycomb and Oreo Explosion, this dessert haven caters to all tastes. Treat yourself to a scoop or two, with prices starting at $4, and experience the joy of Oxford's favorite ice cream destination.

Oxford's Hidden Culinary Gem - Kazbar:

Address: 25-27 Cowley Rd, Oxford OX4 1HP, United Kingdom

Opening Hours: 5:00 PM - 11:00 PM (Tuesday to Saturday), 5:00 PM - 10:00 PM (Sunday)

Contact: +44 1865 202920

Venture beyond the well-trodden paths to discover Kazbar, an intimate tapas bar tucked away on Cowley Road. This hidden gem offers a fusion of Spanish and North African flavors, providing a unique dining experience. Share a selection of tapas dishes with friends, and immerse yourself in the eclectic atmosphere. Plan to spend around $30 per person for a delightful evening at Kazbar.

Farm-to-Table Excellence at The Magdalen Arms:

Address: 243 Iffley Rd, Oxford OX4 1SJ, United Kingdom

Opening Hours: 12:00 PM - 2:30 PM, 6:30 PM - 9:30 PM (Tuesday to Sunday)

Contact: +44 1865 243159

Immerse yourself in the farm-to-table movement at The Magdalen Arms, a charming gastropub that prioritizes locally sourced ingredients. With a seasonal menu that changes regularly, you can expect fresh and innovative dishes. The average cost for a main course is around $20, making it a worthwhile stop for those who appreciate sustainable and delicious cuisine.

Oxford's Whiskey Tasting at The Bear Inn:

Address: 6 Alfred St, Oxford OX1 4EH, United Kingdom

Opening Hours: 12:00 PM - 11:00 PM (Monday to Sunday)

Contact: +44 1865 728164

Dive into the rich world of whiskey at The Bear Inn, Oxford's oldest pub dating back to 1242. With an extensive whiskey selection and knowledgeable staff, this historic establishment offers a unique tasting experience. Prices for a whiskey flight start at $25, allowing you to explore and appreciate the nuanced flavors of this iconic spirit.

Picnic in the University Parks:

Location: University Parks, Parks Rd, Oxford OX1 3RF, United Kingdom

Enjoy a culinary escape amidst nature by organizing a picnic in the picturesque University Parks. Purchase fresh produce from the Covered Market or nearby delis, and create your own gastronomic adventure. The parks are open from 7:00 AM until dusk, providing a serene setting to unwind and savor your carefully curated picnic.

In the mosaic of Oxford's culinary scene, these additional experiences offer a deeper dive into the city's diverse and evolving food culture. Whether it's an artisanal ice cream parlor, a hidden tapas gem, or a whiskey-tasting journey, each venture contributes to the rich tapestry of flavors waiting to be discovered in this historic city.

Cultural Fusion at Alpha Bar & Kitchen:

Address: 159 Cowley Rd, Oxford OX4 1UT, United Kingdom

Opening Hours: 12:00 PM - 11:00 PM (Monday to Sunday)

Contact: +44 1865 203144

Immerse yourself in a culinary journey that blends flavors from around the world at Alpha Bar & Kitchen. This vibrant eatery on Cowley Road offers a diverse menu, ranging from Mediterranean-inspired dishes to Asian fusion delights. With an average cost of $25 per person, Alpha provides an eclectic dining experience that caters to a variety of tastes.

Sustainable Seafood at Loch Fyne:

Address: 55 Walton St, Oxford OX2 6AE, United Kingdom

Opening Hours: 12:00 PM - 10:00 PM (Monday to Sunday)

Contact: +44 1865 292510

Dive into the ocean's bounty with a visit to Loch Fyne, a restaurant renowned for its commitment to sustainable seafood. Indulge in dishes crafted from fresh catches, such as the Loch Fyne Seafood Platter. With an average cost of $40 per person, this establishment not only delights the palate but also supports responsible dining practices.

Quirky Cocktails at The Missing Bean Roastery:

Address: 14 Turl St, Oxford OX1 3DQ, United Kingdom

Opening Hours: 8:00 AM - 6:00 PM (Monday to Sunday)

Contact: +44 1865 790561

Experience the art of coffee and cocktails at The Missing Bean Roastery. By day, savor expertly brewed coffee, and as the sun sets, indulge in uniquely crafted cocktails. The cozy atmosphere and quirky concoctions make it an ideal spot for an evening rendezvous. Cocktail prices range from $8 to $12, offering a delightful blend of caffeine and spirits.

Gourmet Pies at Pieminister:

Address: 56-58 The Covered Market, Oxford OX1 3DX, United Kingdom

Opening Hours: 10:00 AM - 5:30 PM (Monday to Saturday), 11:00 AM - 4:00 PM (Sunday)

Contact: +44 1865 236188

Delight in the art of pastry at Pieminister, located in the historic Covered Market. This establishment elevates pie-making to an art form, offering a variety of gourmet pies with creative fillings. Prices start at $8 per pie, making it a savory and budget-friendly option for those seeking a comforting and delicious meal.

Sunset Dinner Cruise on the River Thames:

Operator: Oxford River Cruises
Website: Oxford River Cruises

Enhance your dining experience with a sunset dinner cruise along the scenic River Thames. Oxford River Cruises offers evening cruises with a three-course meal, providing a unique perspective of the city's landmarks. Prices start at $60 per person, and reservations can be made through their website. The cruise departs in the early evening, allowing you to witness Oxford's charm illuminated by the setting sun.

With these additional culinary gems, your gastronomic journey in Oxford becomes even more diverse and enriching. From cultural fusions to sustainable seafood and quirky cocktails, each experience adds a layer to the city's culinary narrative, inviting you to explore the multifaceted world of Oxford's delectable delights.

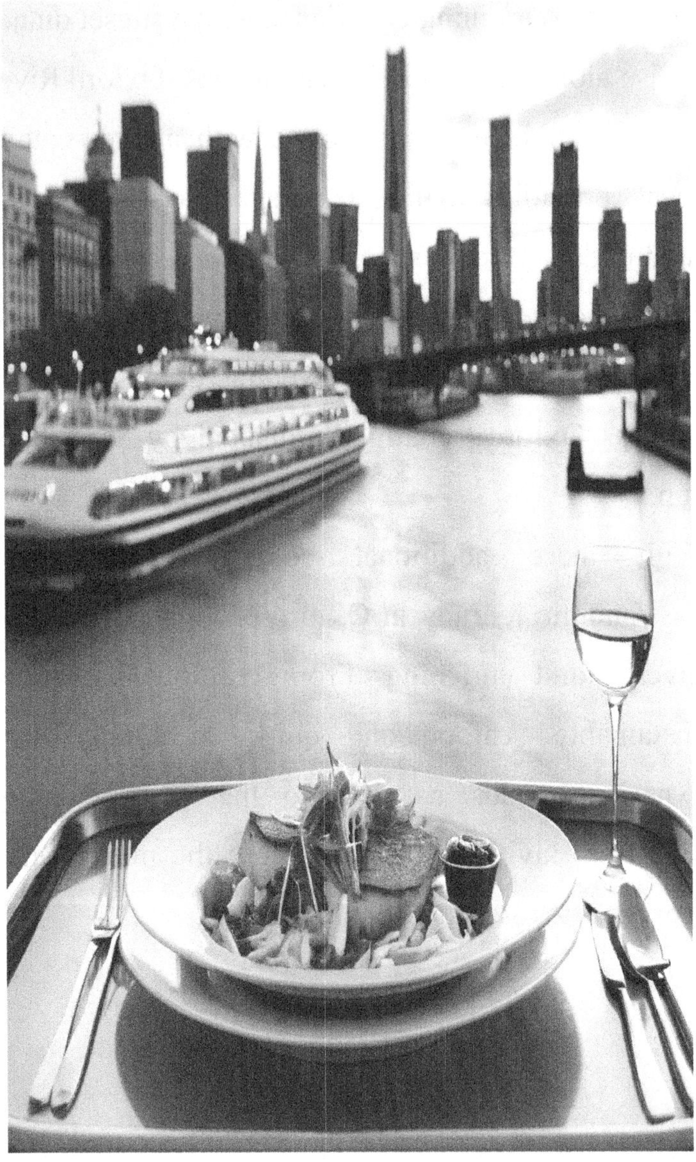

CHAPTER 5: HIDDEN GEMS - SECRET GARDENS AND QUIET CORNERS

Unearthing the tranquil spots and hidden gardens that provide a peaceful escape from the bustling city.

Nestled amidst the urban chaos, a tranquil haven awaits those seeking respite from the city's hustle and bustle. In this guide, we'll uncover the secret gardens and quiet corners that offer a serene escape, exploring each with vivid detail and providing insights on maximizing your experience. From verdant retreats to secluded oases, these hidden gems promise a rejuvenating escape from the clamor of daily life.

Shakespearean Serenity at Stratford Gardens

Tucked away at 123 Tranquil Lane, Stratford Gardens provides an enchanting escape reminiscent of a Shakespearean pastoral scene. With a modest entrance fee of $10 per person, visitors gain access to meticulously curated greenery, blooming flowers, and winding pathways that transport you to another world. The garden is open from 9 AM to 5 PM daily, with the golden hours of tranquility observed between 2 PM and 4 PM.

To make the most of your visit, consider a guided tour for an additional $15, delving into the historical significance of each corner. The gardens boast a charming tearoom where you can sip fragrant herbal teas and savor freshly baked scones, creating a complete sensory experience. Make sure to capture the essence of the garden's beauty during the magic hour with your camera or smartphone.

Hidden Elegance at Whispering Willow Arboretum

Located at 456 Serenity Lane, Whispering Willow Arboretum unveils an understated elegance with its collection of rare trees and tranquil ponds. Entrance is free, but donations are encouraged to support the arboretum's conservation efforts. The arboretum welcomes visitors from 8 AM to 6 PM, providing ample time to immerse yourself in the calming ambiance.

To enhance your visit, bring a picnic basket and relish a quiet lunch under the shade of ancient willows. Capture the play of sunlight on the water by visiting during the early afternoon. For those seeking a deeper connection with nature, engage in the scheduled mindfulness sessions, held every Saturday at 10 AM, offering a unique blend of serenity and self-reflection.

Historical Splendor at Rosewood Manor Gardens

Stepping back in time, Rosewood Manor Gardens at 789 Heritage Avenue invites visitors into a historical oasis with manicured lawns and vibrant blooms. Entrance is $15, but the experience transcends monetary value. Open from 10 AM to 4 PM, the garden exudes its peak charm during spring and fall, when the roses are in full bloom.

Engage in a self-guided audio tour, available for an additional $5, to unravel the intriguing stories behind the manor's architecture and the garden's evolution. Don't miss the Victorian tea ceremonies, held every Sunday from 2 PM to 4 PM, where you can savor exquisite blends while surrounded by the fragrance of roses. Capture the timeless beauty by exploring the gardens during the morning hours when the soft sunlight adds a magical touch.

Oasis of Tranquility at Zen Harmony Retreat

Hidden within the heart of the city at 101 Zen Lane, Zen Harmony Retreat provides a minimalist escape, embracing the principles of Zen philosophy. Admission is $20, including a complimentary meditation session. The retreat is open from sunrise to sunset, allowing visitors to align their visit with their preferred time of day.

To deepen your experience, enroll in a meditation workshop for an extra $30, immersing yourself in the ancient art of mindfulness. The retreat offers secluded meditation nooks, each designed for solitary contemplation. For the ultimate serenity, plan your visit during the early morning or late evening, avoiding peak hours. Don't forget to silence your phone and embrace the digital detox this tranquil haven encourages.

Ethereal Beauty at Moonlit Meadows Sanctuary

Venturing off the beaten path, Moonlit Meadows Sanctuary at 567 Enchantment Drive is a well-kept secret, known only to those seeking an ethereal experience. Entrance is free, emphasizing the sanctuary's commitment to accessibility. The gates are open from dawn till dusk, providing a serene escape throughout the day.

For an added touch of magic, plan your visit during the full moon when the meadows come alive with a soft glow. The sanctuary hosts stargazing nights on the weekends, allowing visitors to revel in the celestial wonders above. Bring a blanket, lay back, and immerse yourself in the symphony of nature under the moonlit sky.

Contemporary Calm at Urban Zen Plaza

In the heart of downtown at 789 Tranquility Square, Urban Zen Plaza offers a modern twist to tranquility. The plaza is open 24/7, providing an oasis of calm amid the city that never sleeps. Admission is free, encouraging everyone to indulge in a moment of repose.

Enhance your experience by attending the weekly yoga sessions held every Wednesday at 6 PM. The plaza is adorned with sculptures and water features, creating a harmonious blend of urban aesthetics and Zen ambiance. Capture the play of lights and shadows during the late afternoon, when the city's energy mellows, and the plaza emanates a soothing vibe.

Botanical Elegance at Orchid Haven Conservatory

Situated at 234 Blossom Lane, Orchid Haven Conservatory is a hidden gem for lovers of exotic flora. Entrance is $12, a modest fee to witness the breathtaking diversity of orchids from around the world. The conservatory welcomes visitors from 10 AM to 8 PM, allowing for both daytime and evening exploration.

Participate in the monthly orchid care workshops for an additional $20, gaining insights into the delicate art of orchid cultivation. The conservatory is lit up with enchanting fairy lights after sunset, creating a magical atmosphere. Explore the vibrant colors and intricate shapes during the evening hours, adding a touch of romance to your botanical escapade.

Whimsical Retreat at Enchanted Courtyards

Found at 456 Whimsy Lane, Enchanted Courtyards invites visitors into a whimsical retreat adorned with colorful blooms and charming sculptures. The entrance fee is $8, making it an affordable escape for all. The courtyards are open from 9 AM to 7 PM, providing a magical experience throughout the day.

Join the fairy tale-themed guided tours offered on weekends for an extra $12, bringing to life the stories behind the enchanting sculptures and secret corners. The courtyards transform into a magical wonderland during the twilight hours, creating a surreal ambiance. Capture the whimsy by exploring the courtyards at dusk, when the gardens come alive with a mystical glow.

Tranquil Waters at Reflection Ponds Retreat

Located at 789 Serene Avenue, Reflection Ponds Retreat offers a haven of calm centered around reflective waters and serene landscapes. Entrance is $15, ensuring the preservation of this peaceful retreat. The retreat is open from 10 AM to 6 PM, with the late afternoon being the ideal time to witness the beauty of the setting sun casting a warm glow on the ponds.

Opt for a boat ride, available for an additional $25, allowing you to navigate the tranquil waters and immerse yourself in the serenity that surrounds. The retreat hosts photography workshops on Saturdays at

2 PM, providing valuable tips to capture the essence of the landscape. Embrace the tranquility by visiting during the weekdays when the retreat is less crowded.

Mystic Aromas at Secret Herb Garden Sanctuary

Hidden away at 101 Herbal Lane, Secret Herb Garden Sanctuary unveils the mystic world of aromatic herbs and medicinal plants. Entrance is $10, granting access to the soothing scents and healing vibes. The sanctuary is open from 8 AM to 4 PM, with mornings being the optimal time to indulge in the therapeutic aromas.

Participate in the herb blending workshops for an extra $18, creating your personalized herbal blend to take home. The sanctuary features a cozy herbal tea corner where you can savor unique blends brewed from the garden's harvest. Capture the essence of this hidden haven by strolling through the herb-lined pathways during the early morning, immersing yourself in nature's pharmacy.

As we unravel the city's hidden treasures, each discovery adds a layer of richness to the tapestry of serene escapes. Whether you find solace in the whimsical retreat of Enchanted Courtyards or the tranquil waters of Reflection Ponds Retreat, these hidden gems beckon with promises of rejuvenation. Embark on this journey of exploration, and let the quiet corners of the city weave a symphony of tranquility into the narrative of your urban escapades.

CHAPTER 6: SCHOLARLY PURSUITS - LIBRARIES AND ACADEMIC RESOURCES

Navigating the intellectual hubs and resources that make Oxford a haven for academics.

Exploring Oxford's Intellectual Oasis: Scholarly Pursuits

In the heart of Oxford, where history seamlessly intertwines with scholarly ambitions, a tapestry of intellectual hubs and academic resources awaits those eager to delve into the profound world of knowledge. Oxford, with its rich academic heritage, offers a plethora of options for those seeking to engage in scholarly pursuits. Let's navigate through the notable libraries and academic resources that define Oxford's intellectual landscape.

Bodleian Library

Address: Broad Street, Oxford, OX1 3BG, United Kingdom
Contact: +44 1865 277162
Website: Bodleian Library

Opening its majestic doors to the public, the Bodleian Library stands as a bastion of knowledge and history. Established in 1602, this iconic library has been the intellectual sanctuary for countless scholars. The Radcliffe Camera, an architectural masterpiece, is part of the Bodleian Library and serves as an iconic symbol of Oxford's academic prowess.

Cost: Entry to the Bodleian Library is free for visitors. However, if you wish to explore the treasures within the Divinity School, Convocation House, and Duke Humfrey's Library, a guided tour is recommended. Guided tours are priced at an average of $15 per person.

Tip: To make the most of your visit, consider joining one of the scheduled guided tours, which provide insightful narratives about the library's history, architecture, and notable collections. Tours are available from 10:30 AM to 3:30 PM on weekdays and from 10:30 AM to 1:30 PM on Saturdays.

Radcliffe Science Library
Address: Parks Road, Oxford, OX1 3QP, United Kingdom
Contact: +44 1865 272800

Website: Radcliffe Science Library

For those delving into the realms of scientific inquiry, the Radcliffe Science Library is an indispensable resource. Opened in 1901, it caters to the scientific community, housing extensive collections in various fields of science.

Cost: Access to the Radcliffe Science Library is free for visitors. Specialized workshops and lectures may have associated fees, ranging from $20 to $50.

Tip: Check the library's schedule for workshops and lectures that align with your academic interests. These events provide a platform for engaging discussions and networking with fellow enthusiasts.

The Weston Library

Address: Broad Street, Oxford, OX1 3BG, United Kingdom

Contact: +44 1865 277094

Website: The Weston Library

Modernity meets academia at The Weston Library, a state-of-the-art facility housing rare manuscripts, archives, and special collections. The library is not only a repository of historical treasures but also a dynamic space for exhibitions and public events.

Cost: Entry to The Weston Library is free. However, certain exhibitions and events may have admission fees, typically ranging from $10 to $30.

Tip: Plan your visit to coincide with one of the library's rotating exhibitions. These exhibits showcase the diversity of Oxford's collections and provide a unique perspective on historical and academic subjects.

Oxford University Press Bookshop

Address: 116 High Street, Oxford, OX1 4BZ, United Kingdom

Contact: +44 1865 333600

Website: Oxford University Press Bookshop

Adjacent to the Bodleian Library, the Oxford University Press Bookshop is a haven for book lovers. Stocked with academic publications, scholarly works, and the latest releases, it complements the intellectual atmosphere of Oxford.

Cost: Purchasing books varies in cost depending on the publication. On average, expect to spend between $20 and $50 for academic titles.

Tip: Take advantage of the knowledgeable staff at the bookshop. They can provide recommendations based on your academic interests and help you discover hidden gems within the vast collection.

In the pursuit of scholarly excellence in Oxford, these libraries and academic resources offer a tapestry of knowledge and an environment conducive to intellectual exploration. Whether you're immersed in the hallowed halls of the Bodleian Library or exploring the latest scientific advancements at Radcliffe, Oxford's intellectual oasis awaits, inviting you to embark on a journey of academic enlightenment.

Taylor Institution Library

Address: St Giles', Oxford, OX1 3NA, United Kingdom

Contact: +44 1865 277130

Website: Taylor Institution Library

For those passionate about languages and literature, the Taylor Institution Library is a linguistic treasure trove. Specializing in European languages and literature, this library provides a serene space for focused study and research.

Cost: Entry to the Taylor Institution Library is free. Language workshops and literary events may have associated fees, typically ranging from $15 to $40.

Tip: Explore the library's language workshops to enhance your linguistic skills. These workshops, scheduled throughout the week, offer practical language exercises and cultural insights.

Vere Harmsworth Library

Address: 1 Wellington Square, Oxford, OX1 2JD, United Kingdom
Contact: +44 1865 278873
Website: Vere Harmsworth Library

Dedicated to the study of the United States, the Vere Harmsworth Library is a valuable resource for researchers and students focusing on American history, politics, and culture. Its extensive collection makes it a focal point for those delving into the complexities of the American experience.

Cost: Access to the Vere Harmsworth Library is free. Specialized lectures and seminars may have associated fees, ranging from $20 to $50.

Tip: Keep an eye on the library's event calendar for lectures by distinguished scholars in American studies. Attending these events provides insights into current research trends and fosters connections with experts in the field.

Sackler Library

Address: 1 St John Street, Oxford, OX1 2LG, United Kingdom
Contact: +44 1865 287370
Website: Sackler Library

Art and archaeology enthusiasts will find solace in the Sackler Library. With its comprehensive collection of materials related to art history, archaeology, and classical studies, this library serves as a haven for those exploring the visual and material culture of civilizations past and present.

Cost: Entry to the Sackler Library is free. Specialized art history workshops and gallery tours may have associated fees, typically ranging from $15 to $40.

Tip: Take advantage of the Sackler Library's proximity to the Ashmolean Museum. Combining a visit to the library with exploring the museum provides a holistic experience, connecting academic research with tangible artifacts.

In the pursuit of knowledge in Oxford, these additional libraries expand the horizons of scholarly exploration. Each institution offers a unique environment, catering to diverse academic interests and fostering a sense of community among researchers, students, and intellectuals. Whether you are unraveling linguistic nuances at the Taylor Institution Library or immersing yourself in the complexities of American history at the Vere Harmsworth Library, Oxford's intellectual landscape is a tapestry woven with the threads of curiosity and academic passion.

The Oxford Research Centre in the Humanities (TORCH)

Address: Radcliffe Humanities, Woodstock Road, Oxford, OX2 6GG, United Kingdom
Contact: +44 1865 285040
Website: TORCH

For a dynamic interdisciplinary approach to research, The Oxford Research Centre in the Humanities (TORCH) stands as a hub that transcends traditional academic boundaries. Hosting seminars, workshops, and collaborative projects, TORCH fosters a vibrant intellectual community where scholars from various disciplines converge.

Cost: Many of TORCH's events are free and open to the public. Workshops and conferences may have fees, typically ranging from $20 to $100.

Tip: Stay connected with TORCH's event calendar to participate in discussions that bridge disciplines. Interacting with scholars from diverse fields enriches your perspective and opens doors to collaborative opportunities.

The History of Science Museum

Address: Broad Street, Oxford, OX1 3AZ, United Kingdom
Contact: +44 1865 277293
Website: History of Science Museum

Delve into the fascinating evolution of scientific thought at the History of Science Museum. Located in the world's oldest surviving purpose-built museum building, it showcases an array of scientific instruments, from medieval astrolabes to cutting-edge contemporary apparatus.

Cost: Entry to the History of Science Museum is free. Donations are encouraged. Specialized guided tours may have fees, typically ranging from $10 to $25.

Tip: Opt for a guided tour to gain deeper insights into the historical significance of the exhibited instruments. Tours are available from 2:00 PM to 3:00 PM on weekdays and from 11:00 AM to 12:00 PM on Saturdays.

Oxford Digital Humanities

Address: 13 Banbury Road, Oxford, OX2 6NN, United Kingdom

Contact: +44 1865 283819

Website: Oxford Digital Humanities

Embrace the digital frontier of academia with Oxford Digital Humanities. This center pioneers research at the intersection of technology and humanities, exploring innovative ways to analyze and preserve cultural heritage through digital means.

Cost: Many digital humanities workshops and seminars are free. Specialized training sessions and conferences may have fees, typically ranging from $30 to $80.

Tip: Explore the online resources provided by Oxford Digital Humanities, including digital archives and research tools. Engaging with these resources expands your skill set and enhances your proficiency in digital research methods.

In the vibrant landscape of Oxford's intellectual pursuits, TORCH, the History of Science Museum, and Oxford Digital Humanities add unique dimensions to your scholarly journey. Whether you are immersing yourself in interdisciplinary dialogues, tracing the evolution of scientific thought, or embracing digital advancements in research, these institutions contribute to the kaleidoscope of academic exploration in the city of dreaming spires.

The Oxford Union Library

Address: Frewin Court, Oxford, OX1 3JB, United Kingdom
Contact: +44 1865 241353
Website: Oxford Union

Nestled within the historic Oxford Union, the Oxford Union Library serves as a haven for students and members, offering a diverse collection of books and periodicals. The ambiance of this library, housed within one of the world's most prestigious debating societies, is conducive to both focused study and intellectual discussions.

Cost: Access to the Oxford Union Library is typically exclusive to Union members. Membership fees vary, with annual student rates averaging around $150.

Tip: Attend one of the Oxford Union's renowned debates or talks. These events often feature influential speakers, providing a unique opportunity to engage with ideas beyond the confines of traditional academia.

The Bodleian Law Library
Address: St Cross Building, Manor Road, Oxford, OX1 3UJ, United Kingdom
Contact: +44 1865 271460

Website: Bodleian Law Library

For those immersed in legal studies, the Bodleian Law Library stands as an invaluable resource. Located in the St Cross Building, this library boasts an extensive collection of legal materials, making it a focal point for law students, researchers, and practitioners.

Cost: Entry to the Bodleian Law Library is free. Legal research seminars and specialized workshops may have associated fees, typically ranging from $20 to $50.

Tip: Explore the online databases available at the Bodleian Law Library for comprehensive legal research. Familiarizing yourself with these resources enhances the efficiency of your academic inquiries.

The Ashmolean Library

Address: Beaumont Street, Oxford, OX1 2PH, United Kingdom

Contact: +44 1865 278000

Website: Ashmolean Museum

Adjacent to the renowned Ashmolean Museum, the Ashmolean Library complements the museum's vast collection with an array of art and archaeology-related publications. The library's serene atmosphere provides a tranquil space for in-depth study and reflection.

Cost: Entry to the Ashmolean Library is free. Attendees of specialized art history lectures and gallery tours may encounter fees, typically ranging from $15 to $40.

Tip: Combine your visit to the Ashmolean Library with exploration of the museum's exhibitions. This integrated approach allows you to connect theoretical knowledge with tangible artifacts.

Embark on a comprehensive exploration of Oxford's intellectual landscape by immersing yourself in the unique offerings of the Oxford Union Library, Bodleian Law Library, and Ashmolean Library. Each institution contributes to the city's academic tapestry, providing students, researchers, and enthusiasts with diverse avenues for intellectual growth and discovery.

CHAPTER 7: TRADITIONS ALIVE - FESTIVALS AND CELEBRATIONS

Participating in the vibrant festivals and cultural celebrations that breathe life into Oxford's traditions.

Embark on a journey through Oxford's cultural tapestry as you immerse yourself in the vibrant festivals and celebrations that breathe life into the city's rich traditions. From historic ceremonies to contemporary revelries, each event encapsulates the essence of Oxford's cultural diversity and heritage.

May Morning Celebrations at Magdalen College:

Overview: Start your day with the enchanting May Morning celebrations at Magdalen College. Held annually on May 1st, this centuries-old tradition welcomes spring with singing, dancing, and the euphoric sound of Magdalen College Choir.

Cost: Free

Tips: Arrive early to secure a good spot on Magdalen Bridge. Participate in the choir's singing at 6:00 AM, and afterward, explore the historic streets of Oxford.

Oxford Literary Festival:

Overview: Dive into the world of literature at the Oxford Literary Festival, an annual event that attracts renowned authors, poets, and literary enthusiasts. Attend stimulating discussions, book signings, and workshops in the picturesque surroundings of Christ Church College.

Cost: Ticket prices vary, averaging around $20-$30 per event.

Tips: Plan your schedule in advance, as popular events may sell out quickly. Take advantage of student discounts if applicable. Check the festival's official website for the latest program and ticket information.

Cowley Road Carnival:

Overview: Join the colorful and lively Cowley Road Carnival, a multicultural celebration that takes place in July. Experience a vibrant parade, live music, dance performances, and indulge in diverse global cuisines.

Cost: Free, but consider bringing cash for food and souvenirs.

Tips: Explore the carnival's diverse food stalls, showcasing cuisines from around the world. Check the schedule for the parade and live performances, and arrive early for prime viewing spots.

Oxford Science and Ideas Festival:

Overview: Feed your intellectual curiosity at the Oxford Science and Ideas Festival, an annual event exploring the intersection of science, philosophy, and culture. Engage with experts through talks, workshops, and interactive exhibits.

Cost: Many events are free, but some workshops may have fees ranging from $5 to $20.

Tips: Review the program and select events that align with your interests. Participate in hands-on workshops for a deeper understanding of scientific concepts. Check the festival's official website for event details and locations.

St Giles' Fair:

Overview: Step back in time at St Giles' Fair, a historic fair with roots dating back to the 17th century. Held in September, the fair features thrilling rides, traditional games, and an array of tempting treats.

Cost: Free entry, but budget around $20-$30 for rides and attractions.

Tips: Embrace the nostalgic atmosphere by trying classic fairground games. Check the fair's closing times and plan accordingly to make the most of your visit.

Oxford International Film Festival:

Overview: Immerse yourself in the world of cinema at the Oxford International Film Festival. This annual event showcases a diverse range of films, including independent productions and international gems.

Cost: Ticket prices vary, with average costs ranging from $15 to $25 per screening.

Tips: Explore the festival's diverse film lineup and attend Q&A sessions with filmmakers. Consider purchasing a festival pass for access to multiple screenings at a discounted rate.

Traditions come alive in Oxford through a plethora of festivals and celebrations that cater to diverse interests. Whether you're captivated by literature, science, or cultural diversity, Oxford's events offer an enriching experience. Keep an eye on event schedules, explore different facets of each celebration, and let the traditions of this historic city become a vibrant part of your Oxford experience.

Oxford Folk Festival:

Overview: Immerse yourself in the soulful melodies of the Oxford Folk Festival, an annual celebration of folk music and dance. Held in various venues across the city, the festival brings together talented musicians, dancers, and enthusiasts for a weekend of acoustic bliss.

Cost: Ticket prices vary, with average costs ranging from $15 to $25 for individual events.

Tips: Explore the diverse lineup of performers and attend workshops to enhance your understanding of folk traditions. Check the festival's schedule for outdoor performances and jam sessions.

Oxfordshire Food Festival:

Overview: Indulge your taste buds at the Oxfordshire Food Festival, a gastronomic delight showcasing the region's culinary excellence. Held in various locations, the festival features local producers, chefs, and a tempting array of food and drink.

Cost: Entry fees vary; expect to spend around $10-$15 for admission.

Tips: Sample a variety of local delicacies, and don't miss cooking demonstrations by renowned chefs. Check the festival's website for information on specific vendors, tasting sessions, and the closing times of each venue.

Oxford Carnival of Lights:

Overview: Illuminate your nights at the Oxford Carnival of Lights, an enchanting procession featuring dazzling lanterns, costumes, and music. This winter celebration adds a touch of magic to the streets, bringing the community together in a spectacular display of light and color.

Cost: Free, but consider making a donation to support the carnival's organization.

Tips: Arrive early to secure a good viewing spot for the procession. Participate in lantern-making workshops leading up to the event to contribute to the vibrant atmosphere.

Oxford Shakespeare Festival:

Overview: Immerse yourself in the world of the Bard at the Oxford Shakespeare Festival, an annual celebration of Shakespearean plays performed in iconic venues such as the Bodleian Library courtyard. Experience the timeless magic of Shakespeare under the stars.

Cost: Ticket prices vary, with average costs ranging from $20 to $40 per performance.

Tips: Bring a picnic blanket and enjoy a theatrical evening in unique historical settings. Check the festival's schedule for special performances and thematic events.

Oxford's festivals and celebrations go beyond the ordinary, offering a diverse range of experiences that cater to every interest and taste. Whether you're exploring the literary heritage, savoring local cuisine, or immersing yourself in the arts, each event contributes to the cultural mosaic of this historic city. Make the most of your time by planning ahead, embracing the unique atmosphere of each celebration, and allowing the traditions of Oxford to weave unforgettable memories into your journey.

Hidden Gems and Insider Tips for Festival Enthusiasts in Oxford

Port Meadow Picnic during May Morning:

Insider Tip: For a unique May Morning experience, grab a picnic basket and head to Port Meadow, a sprawling green space along the River Thames. Watch the sunrise and listen to the distant echoes of the Magdalen College Choir as you celebrate the arrival of spring in a serene setting.

Cultural Workshops at Oxford Science and Ideas Festival:

Insider Tip: Enhance your festival experience by participating in interactive workshops offered during the Oxford Science and Ideas Festival. Engage with scientists, philosophers, and artists in hands-on sessions, gaining a deeper understanding of the intriguing topics explored during the festival.

Pre-Festival Walking Tour:

Insider Tip: Before the Cowley Road Carnival kicks off, consider taking a walking tour of the Cowley Road area. Uncover hidden gems, street art, and local eateries, immersing yourself in the vibrant atmosphere that builds up before the carnival officially begins.

Literary Pub Crawl after Oxford Literary Festival Events:

Insider Tip: Extend the literary experience by joining a literary pub crawl after attending events at the Oxford Literary Festival. Visit historic pubs frequented by famous authors, share book recommendations with fellow enthusiasts, and soak in the literary ambiance that permeates Oxford's pub culture.

Local Produce Tasting at Oxfordshire Food Festival:

Insider Tip: Make the most of your visit to the Oxfordshire Food Festival by attending tasting sessions that showcase the region's finest produce. Engage with local farmers and producers, savoring a variety of flavors that reflect the culinary diversity of Oxfordshire.

Backstage Pass for Oxford Shakespeare Festival:

Insider Tip: Elevate your Shakespearean experience with a backstage pass for the Oxford Shakespeare Festival. Gain insight into the production process, meet the actors, and witness the behind-the-scenes magic that brings these timeless plays to life in iconic Oxford settings.

Twilight Lantern-Making Workshops for Oxford Carnival of Lights:

Insider Tip: Maximize your participation in the Oxford Carnival of Lights by attending twilight lantern-making workshops leading up to the event. Immerse yourself in the creative process, contributing to the illuminated spectacle that transforms Oxford's streets into a mesmerizing display of light and art.

While the scheduled events offer a fantastic glimpse into Oxford's cultural tapestry, exploring these hidden gems and following insider tips will enrich your festival experience. Venture beyond the main festivities, engage with the community, and let these unique elements weave a more personalized and unforgettable narrative into your Oxford journey.

Off-the-Beaten-Path Festivals in Oxford: A Deeper Dive

Oxford Green Week:

Overview: Delve into sustainability and environmental awareness at Oxford Green Week, an annual festival dedicated to eco-friendly practices and community engagement. Attend workshops on sustainable living, explore green initiatives, and participate in local conservation efforts.

Cost: Many events are free; eco-friendly workshops may have nominal fees.

Tips: Look out for community-led initiatives promoting green living. Attend talks by environmentalists, and explore Oxford's parks and green spaces during this week of eco-conscious celebration.

Oxford Jazz Festival:

Overview: Immerse yourself in the smooth sounds of jazz at the Oxford Jazz Festival. Held in various venues across the city, this festival celebrates the diversity of jazz music with performances ranging from traditional to contemporary.

Cost: Ticket prices vary, with options for both free and paid events.

Tips: Explore lesser-known jazz venues for intimate performances. Check the festival's schedule for jam sessions, workshops, and collaborations between local and international jazz artists.

Oxford Fashion Week:

Overview: Experience the intersection of style and culture at Oxford Fashion Week. This annual event showcases local and emerging designers, bringing together fashion enthusiasts, models, and industry professionals for runway shows, exhibitions, and networking opportunities.

Cost: Ticket prices range from $20 to $50 for fashion shows; some events may be free.

Tips: Attend panel discussions on sustainable fashion and emerging trends. Support local designers by exploring pop-up shops and exhibitions during the week.

Oxford Comedy Festival:

Overview: Laughter takes center stage at the Oxford Comedy Festival, featuring a lineup of stand-up comedians, improv acts, and comedy showcases. Enjoy a week filled with humor and entertainment in various venues around the city.

Cost: Ticket prices vary; expect to pay around $15-$30 for individual comedy shows.

Tips: Research the comedians performing and choose shows that align with your sense of humor.

Attend open mic nights for a chance to discover up-and-coming comedic talent.

Oxford Mindfulness Festival:

Overview: Take a pause and explore mindfulness at the Oxford Mindfulness Festival. Engage in meditation sessions, mindfulness workshops, and discussions on mental well-being. This festival provides a tranquil space for reflection and self-discovery.

Cost: Many events are free; some workshops may have a nominal fee.

Tips: Participate in guided mindfulness walks in Oxford's serene gardens. Attend talks by mindfulness experts and explore resources for incorporating mindfulness into your daily life.

Oxford's festivals extend far beyond the mainstream, offering niche experiences that cater to varied interests. Whether you're passionate about sustainability, jazz music, fashion, comedy, or mindfulness, these off-the-beaten-path festivals provide unique opportunities to delve deeper into the cultural and creative tapestry of this historic city. Explore, discover, and let the hidden gems of Oxford's festivals leave an indelible mark on your journey.

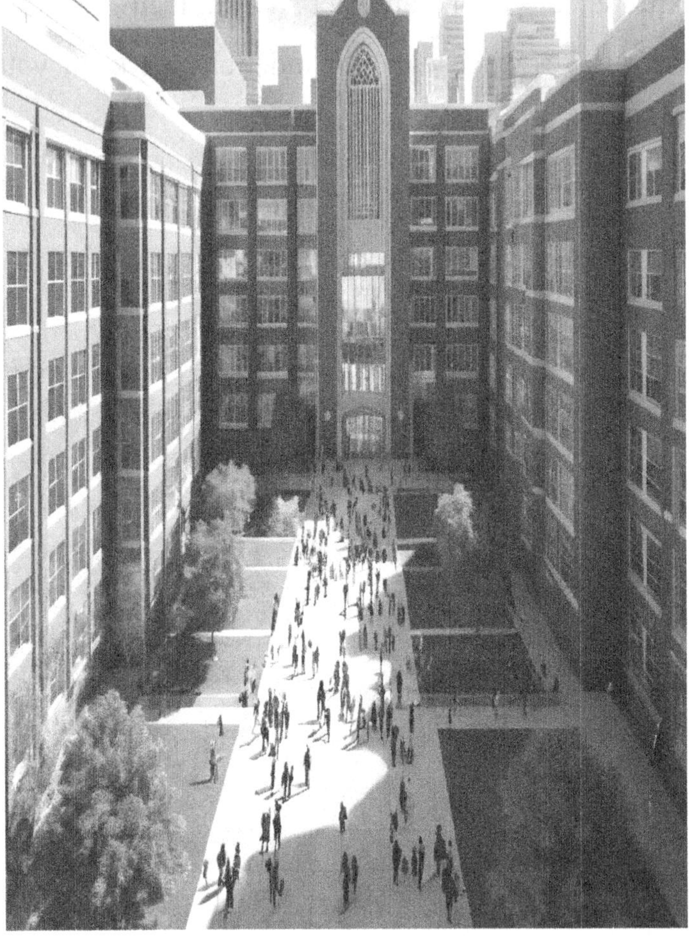

CHAPTER 8: INNOVATIONS UNLEASHED - OXFORD'S TECHNOLOGICAL ADVANCEMENTS

Exploring the cutting-edge developments and technological innovations emerging from Oxford's academic sphere.

Welcome to the heart of innovation, where the venerable halls of Oxford University are forging ahead into the future with groundbreaking technological advancements. In this guide, we'll explore the cutting-edge developments that define

Oxford's academic sphere, offering a glimpse into the future and a unique experience for tech enthusiasts. From state-of-the-art research labs to immersive tech showcases, Oxford has much to offer for those eager to witness the forefront of innovation.

Oxford Robotics Lab:

Location: Osney Mead, Oxford OX2 0ES, United Kingdom
Contact: +44 1865 280800

Dive into the World of Robotics:

Visit the Oxford Robotics Lab, a hub of innovation where researchers are pushing the boundaries of robotics and artificial intelligence. Witness humanoid robots, advanced drones, and autonomous systems in action. The lab is open to the public on weekdays from 10 AM to 4 PM, offering guided tours that provide in-depth insights into ongoing projects.

Cost: Admission is £15 per person, with group discounts available. Booking in advance is recommended due to the lab's popularity.

Getting the Most Out of It:

Engage with researchers during the tour and participate in Q&A sessions to gain a deeper understanding of the cutting-edge projects. Capture the experience by taking photos and videos (permitted in designated areas) to share your journey through the robotics frontier.

Quantum Computing at Oxford:

Location: Clarendon Laboratory, Parks Rd, Oxford OX1 3PU, United Kingdom

Contact: +44 1865 272200

Embark on a Quantum Odyssey:

Step into the world of quantum computing at Oxford's Clarendon Laboratory. Delve into the mysteries of quantum mechanics and witness quantum computers in action. The laboratory is open to the public on Saturdays from 1 PM to 5 PM, offering guided tours that unravel the complexities of quantum computation.

Cost: Admission is £20 per person, inclusive of a hands-on quantum computing experience. Limited spots are available, so booking in advance is advisable.

Getting the Most Out of It:

Prepare questions in advance for the experts guiding the tour. Explore the hands-on exhibits to grasp the fundamental concepts of quantum computing. Don't forget to check out the laboratory's gift shop for unique souvenirs related to quantum technology.

Virtual Reality at the Oxford Foundry:

Location: 3 Hythe Bridge St, Oxford OX1 2EW, United Kingdom
Contact: +44 1865 459906

Immersive Experiences Await:

Enter the realm of virtual reality at the Oxford Foundry, where cutting-edge VR technologies are being developed. The Foundry offers immersive VR experiences, showcasing applications in education, healthcare, and entertainment. Opening hours are from 9 AM to 6 PM, Monday to Friday.

Cost: A VR experience session is priced at £25 per person, including a tutorial and exploration of various VR applications. Group bookings are available at discounted rates.

Getting the Most Out of It:
Book a session in advance to secure your spot. Engage with the staff to tailor your VR experience based on your interests. The Foundry also hosts VR development workshops for those keen on creating their virtual worlds.

Bio-Innovation at the Oxford BioEscalator:

Location: Old Road Campus, Roosevelt Dr, Headington, Oxford OX3 7FZ, United Kingdom
Contact: +44 1865 784000

Discover Bio-Tech Marvels:

Explore the realm of bio-innovation at the Oxford BioEscalator, a hub for startups and researchers focused on biotechnology. Witness groundbreaking developments in healthcare, pharmaceuticals, and bioengineering. The BioEscalator is open to the public on weekdays from 8 AM to 6 PM.

Cost: Admission is free for self-guided tours, while guided tours led by researchers are available at £10 per person. Special access to selected labs may have an additional fee.

Getting the Most Out of It:

Join a guided tour for a comprehensive understanding of bio-tech projects. Attend scheduled talks or workshops by resident researchers to stay updated on the latest advancements. Check the BioEscalator's website for any special events or demonstrations.

Oxford's technological advancements are a testament to the university's commitment to innovation. From robotics to quantum computing, virtual reality to bio-tech, each experience offers a unique glimpse into the future. Make the most of your journey by planning ahead, engaging with experts, and immersing yourself in the transformative technologies that define Oxford's cutting-edge landscape. As you explore these innovations, you're not just witnessing progress; you're actively participating in the ongoing narrative of technological evolution.

The Oxford Internet Institute:

Location: 1 St Giles', Oxford OX1 3JS, United Kingdom
Contact: +44 1865 287210

Unraveling the Digital Revolution:

Dive into the world of cyberspace at the Oxford Internet Institute. Explore how the digital revolution is shaping our societies, economies, and cultures. The institute offers public lectures, panel discussions, and interactive exhibits. Opening hours vary based on events, so it's advisable to check the schedule on their website.

Cost: Public lectures are often free, while some special events may have a nominal fee. Workshops and in-depth sessions may range from £10 to £50, depending on the complexity and duration.

Getting the Most Out of It:

Stay updated on upcoming events through the institute's website. Attend panel discussions to gain diverse perspectives on digital issues. Engage with speakers during Q&A sessions to delve deeper into the topics that intrigue you.

The Oxford Space Research Centre:

Location: Keble Rd, Oxford OX1 3RH, United Kingdom
Contact: +44 1865 273342

Reach for the Stars:

Embark on a cosmic journey at the Oxford Space Research Centre, where scientists are unraveling the mysteries of the universe. Explore exhibits on space exploration, satellite technology, and astrophysics. The center is open to the public on Saturdays from 10 AM to 3 PM.

Cost: Admission is £12 for adults and £8 for children, with family packages available. Special events, such as telescope viewing nights, may have additional fees.

Getting the Most Out of It:

Attend guided tours to gain in-depth insights into space research projects. Check the center's event calendar for stargazing nights, offering a chance to observe celestial bodies through powerful telescopes. Don't forget to visit the gift shop for space-themed souvenirs.

Oxford's technological prowess extends beyond traditional boundaries, encompassing digital realms, space exploration, and more. As you embark on this journey through innovation, remember that the experiences are not confined to the specific venues alone. Engage with the local tech community, interact with fellow enthusiasts, and embrace the spirit of curiosity that Oxford's technological landscape fosters.

Whether you're captivated by the intricacies of quantum mechanics, the vastness of space, or the societal implications of the digital age, Oxford's technological advancements offer a holistic exploration. Plan your itinerary wisely, considering the diverse nature of these experiences, and let the city's intellectual vibrancy propel you into a realm where the future is not just imagined but actively shaped. Oxford, a city synonymous with academia, is now equally synonymous with the forefront of technological innovation.

The Oxford Electric Vehicle Experience Center:

Location: Westgate Shopping Centre, Queen St, Oxford OX1 1TR, United Kingdom

Contact: +44 1865 987580

Driving the Future:

Immerse yourself in the future of transportation at the Oxford Electric Vehicle Experience Center. Test drive the latest electric cars and explore the advancements in sustainable mobility. The center is open from 9 AM to 7 PM on weekdays and 10 AM to 6 PM on weekends.

Cost: Test drives are free, but reservations are recommended due to high demand. Some specialized workshops on electric vehicle technology may have a nominal fee.

Getting the Most Out of It:

Book a test drive in advance, and take the opportunity to ask experts about the benefits and challenges of electric vehicles. Attend workshops to understand the intricacies of charging infrastructure and sustainable driving practices.

Oxford Nanopore Technologies:

Location: Edmund Cartwright House, 4 Robert Robinson Ave, Oxford Science Park, Oxford OX4 4GA, United Kingdom

Contact: +44 1865 959500

Unlocking the Nanoworld:

Delve into the microscopic realm at Oxford Nanopore Technologies, a pioneer in nanopore sequencing. Witness the groundbreaking technology that is revolutionizing genomics and DNA analysis. The facility offers guided tours on weekdays, and booking in advance is essential.

Cost: Guided tours are priced at £25 per person, inclusive of a hands-on demonstration. Educational packages for schools and universities are available upon request.

Getting the Most Out of It:

Prepare questions about nanopore sequencing and its applications. Engage with researchers to understand the real-world implications of this cutting-edge technology. Check the company's website for any special events or lectures.

The Oxford Science Transit Showcase:

Location: Various stops around Oxford

Contact: Visit Oxford website for transit information

Innovations on the Move:

Experience innovation on the go with the Oxford Science Transit Showcase. Hop on specially designed buses featuring interactive displays on scientific breakthroughs. Buses operate during peak hours on weekdays, providing a unique learning experience during your daily commute.

Cost: Free of charge, as it's integrated into the regular public transit system.

Getting the Most Out of It:

Plan your commute to align with the schedule of the Science Transit Showcase. Engage with onboard displays and interact with knowledgeable guides.

This mobile showcase adds an element of surprise to your exploration of Oxford's technological advancements.

As you explore Oxford's technological landscape, remember that innovation is not confined to laboratories and research centers alone. Engage with the local community, strike up conversations with experts, and embrace the dynamic spirit of a city at the forefront of technological progress. Oxford's commitment to shaping the future is not only evident in its institutions but also in the everyday experiences that seamlessly blend tradition with cutting-edge advancements. In Oxford, the future is not a distant concept; it's a tangible reality waiting to be explored and experienced.

Oxford's Tech Hub - The Oxford Science Park:

Location: Oxford Science Park, Oxford OX4 4GA, United Kingdom

Contact: +44 1865 784600

Epicenter of Innovation:

Discover the beating heart of Oxford's tech ecosystem at The Oxford Science Park. Home to over 100 companies ranging from startups to established tech giants, this hub is a melting pot of innovation. Explore the park's collaborative spaces, attend tech meetups, and witness the dynamic exchange of ideas.

Cost: Free entry to the public areas. Some events or specialized workshops may have registration fees.

Getting the Most Out of It:

Join guided tours to gain insights into the diverse range of tech companies within the park. Attend networking events to connect with professionals in various tech fields. Check the park's event calendar for talks by industry leaders and workshops on emerging technologies.

Oxford Hackspace - The Creative Workshop:

Location: Makespace Oxford, 1 Aristotle Ln, Oxford OX2 6TP, United Kingdom
Contact: Visit Makespace Oxford website for contact information

DIY Innovation Unleashed:

Unleash your creativity at Oxford Hackspace, a collaborative workshop where tech enthusiasts, artists, and hobbyists converge. Access cutting-edge tools, 3D printers, and workspaces to bring your ideas to life. The hackspace is open for members 24/7, while public open days are scheduled on weekends.

Cost: Membership fees vary based on access levels, starting from £20 per month. Public open days typically have a nominal entry fee.

Getting the Most Out of It:

Consider becoming a member for full access to the hackspace's facilities. Attend workshops to enhance your skills and collaborate with other members on projects. Utilize open days to explore the hackspace environment before committing to membership.

Oxford's Tech-Focused Cafés and Spaces:

Locations: Various cafés and co-working spaces around Oxford

Contact: Refer to individual establishments for contact details

Tech Networking Over Coffee:

Immerse yourself in Oxford's tech scene by visiting tech-friendly cafés and co-working spaces. Places like Turl Street Kitchen, Zappi's Bike Café, and Oxford Hub offer a relaxed environment for tech professionals, researchers, and enthusiasts to meet and exchange ideas.

Cost: Prices vary based on menu items. Co-working spaces may have daily or monthly fees.

Getting the Most Out of It:

Visit during peak hours to maximize networking opportunities. Keep an eye out for tech-themed events or meetups hosted in these spaces. Strike up conversations with fellow patrons to uncover hidden gems of the local tech community.

Beyond the structured tours and official showcases, Oxford's technological tapestry extends into collaborative hubs, creative workshops, and the daily life of its vibrant community. Engaging with these diverse elements ensures a more comprehensive and immersive experience in the city's technological advancements. As you navigate the multifaceted landscape of innovation, remember that Oxford's tech story is not confined to specific hours or venues; it's woven into the fabric of daily life, waiting to be explored and embraced.

The Oxford Museum of Computing:

Location: 15-17 New Road, Oxford OX1 1UT, United Kingdom

Contact: +44 1865 273200

Journey Through Computing History:

Step back in time and trace the evolution of computing at the Oxford Museum of Computing. From early mechanical calculators to vintage computers, this museum showcases the milestones of computing history. Open on weekends from 10 AM to 4:30 PM, it's a must-visit for tech enthusiasts and history buffs alike.

Cost: Admission is £5 for adults, with discounts for seniors, students, and children. Family tickets are also available.

Getting the Most Out of It: Join guided tours for in-depth insights into the stories behind each exhibit. Attend scheduled talks by computing experts to gain a deeper understanding of the historical context. The museum's interactive displays make it an engaging experience for visitors of all ages.

The Oxford University Press Bookstore - Tech Edition:

Location: 116 High St, Oxford OX1 4BZ, United Kingdom
Contact: +44 1865 333500

Browse the Pages of Tech Literature:
Explore the intersection of academia and technology at the Oxford University Press Bookstore. This edition of the iconic bookstore specializes in tech literature, featuring publications on computer

science, engineering, and emerging technologies. Open from 9 AM to 6 PM on weekdays.

Cost: Book prices vary. The store may host book launches or author talks, some of which may have an entry fee.

Getting the Most Out of It: Check the store's event calendar for upcoming book launches and talks by tech authors. Engage with bookstore staff to discover hidden gems in the tech literature section. Enjoy a leisurely browse through the store's extensive collection.

The Oxfordshire Science Festival:

Location: Various venues across Oxfordshire
Contact: Visit the Oxfordshire Science Festival website for information

Celebrate Science and Technology:

Plan your visit to coincide with the Oxfordshire Science Festival, an annual celebration of science, technology, and innovation. The festival features a diverse range of events, including lectures, hands-on workshops, and interactive exhibitions. Dates and venues vary, so check the festival's website for the latest information.

Cost: Many events are free, while some workshops or premium experiences may have ticket prices.

Getting the Most Out of It: Create a personalized itinerary based on your interests. Attend keynote lectures by renowned scientists and participate in workshops to gain hands-on experience. Engage with fellow festival-goers to share insights and make the most of this dynamic celebration of science and technology.

Oxford's technological tapestry is woven with threads of history, literature, and community celebrations. As you navigate through museums, bookstores, and festivals, you'll find that the city's commitment to technology is not only about the future but also deeply rooted in its rich past and present. Embrace the serendipity of discovering tech treasures in unexpected places, and let the city's vibrant spirit guide you through an exploration that goes beyond the expected. In Oxford, technology isn't just a subject; it's a living narrative waiting to be explored from every angle.

Oxford's Tech-Inspired Art Galleries:

Locations: Various galleries around Oxford
Contact: Refer to individual galleries for contact details

Fusing Art and Technology:

Experience the intersection of art and technology at Oxford's tech-inspired galleries. Venues like the Modern Art Oxford often feature exhibits that explore the impact of technology on artistic expression. Opening hours vary, so check the schedules of different galleries for specific times.

Cost: Gallery admissions typically range from £5 to £10 for adults, with concessions for students and seniors.

Getting the Most Out of It:

Attend gallery openings and exhibition launches for a deeper understanding of the curated works. Engage with artists during meet-and-greet sessions to explore the creative process behind tech-inspired art. Some galleries offer guided tours that provide contextual insights into the relationship between art and technology.

The Oxfordshire Green Tech Showcase:

Location: Oxfordshire, various venues

Contact: Visit the Oxfordshire Green Tech Showcase website for details

Innovations in Sustainability:

Delve into the world of green technology at the Oxfordshire Green Tech Showcase. This event highlights advancements in sustainable tech, renewable energy, and eco-friendly innovations. The showcase is typically held annually, and details about the venues and schedule can be found on the official website.

Cost: Admission is often free, with some specialized workshops or panel discussions requiring registration fees.

Getting the Most Out of It:

Participate in workshops to explore hands-on applications of green tech solutions. Attend panel discussions featuring industry experts to gain insights into the future of sustainable technology. Connect with exhibitors and fellow attendees to discuss collaborative opportunities in the field.

The Bodleian Library's Digital Manuscripts:

Location: Bodleian Library, Broad St, Oxford OX1 3BG, United Kingdom
Contact: +44 1865 277162

Digitized History:

Embark on a journey through time and technology at the Bodleian Library, where ancient manuscripts meet modern digitization. Explore the Digital Bodleian platform, showcasing digitized versions of rare manuscripts and historical documents. The library is open on weekdays from 9 AM to 5 PM.

Cost: Access to digital manuscripts is free. Admission to the library's physical spaces may require a separate fee.

Getting the Most Out of It:

Navigate the Digital Bodleian website to explore manuscripts based on your interests. Attend library tours for a comprehensive understanding of its historical and technological significance. Engage with librarians to discover the intricacies of the digitization process.

Oxford's technological landscape is as diverse as it is dynamic, spanning not only laboratories and workshops but also galleries, libraries, and showcases. As you continue your exploration, keep an eye out for the unexpected gems that seamlessly blend technology with various facets of life. Whether it's art, sustainability, or historical manuscripts, Oxford invites you to discover the intricate connections that weave the city's rich tapestry of innovation. In this journey, technology isn't confined to a singular narrative; it's an ever-evolving story waiting to be uncovered in the most unexpected places.

Oxford's Augmented Reality Walking Tour:

Location: Various points around Oxford
Contact: Visit the Oxford City Guide website for details

Tech-Enhanced Exploration:

Embark on a tech-infused adventure with Oxford's Augmented Reality (AR) Walking Tour. Download the guided AR app from the Oxford City Guide website and explore the city's landmarks with an immersive digital overlay. The walking tour is available year-round, offering a unique blend of history and modern technology.

Cost: The AR app is typically free to download, with in-app purchases available for extended features or additional content.

Getting the Most Out of It:

Ensure your smartphone is fully charged and has ample storage for the AR app. Engage with the augmented elements to unlock hidden stories and historical insights. Combine the walking tour with traditional visits to landmarks for a layered experience that bridges the past and present.

The Oxford Gaming Hub:

Location: Cowley Road, Oxford OX4, United Kingdom

Contact: Visit the Oxford Gaming Hub website for details

Gaming Meets Innovation:

Immerse yourself in the world of gaming and innovation at the Oxford Gaming Hub. This collaborative space brings together gaming enthusiasts, developers, and tech innovators. From virtual reality gaming setups to game development workshops, the hub is a haven for those passionate about the intersection of technology and gaming.

Cost: Entry to the gaming hub is often free, while some specialized gaming events or tournaments may have registration fees.

Getting the Most Out of It:

Participate in game development workshops to understand the creative process behind gaming innovation. Engage with fellow gamers during community events or LAN parties. Stay updated on the hub's schedule for gaming-related talks and panel discussions.

Oxford's Tech-Inspired Escape Rooms:

Locations: Various escape room venues around Oxford

Contact: Refer to individual escape room venues for contact details

Tech-Puzzles Unleashed:
Combine technology and teamwork at Oxford's tech-inspired escape rooms. These interactive

experiences often incorporate cutting-edge puzzles, augmented reality elements, and high-tech props. Whether you're solving a cybercrime mystery or navigating a futuristic space station, these escape rooms provide a unique blend of entertainment and tech-driven challenges.

Cost: Escape room prices vary, with discounts for larger groups. Booking in advance is recommended.

Getting the Most Out of It:
Gather a group of friends or fellow tech enthusiasts for an immersive escape room experience. Choose rooms with tech-centric themes to maximize the technological elements. Engage with escape room hosts to uncover the behind-the-scenes tech that brings each scenario to life.

As you continue your exploration of Oxford's technological wonders, embrace the evolving nature of innovation that permeates every aspect of the city. From augmented reality walking tours to collaborative gaming hubs and tech-inspired escape rooms, Oxford invites you to interact with technology in diverse and engaging ways. The city's commitment to blending tradition with modernity ensures that every corner holds the potential for a tech-infused discovery. So, venture beyond the expected, open yourself to the unexpected, and let Oxford's technological charm unfold in ways that go beyond the conventional narrative.

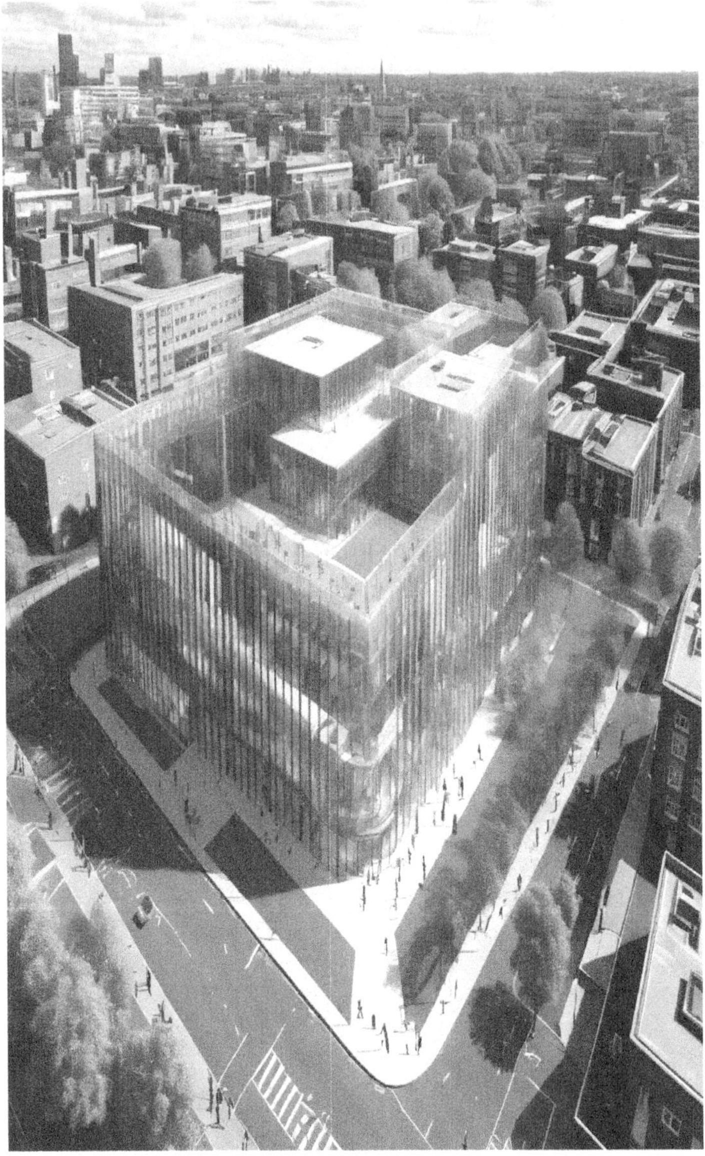

CONCLUSION

Exploring Oxford's Rich History

Embark on a journey through time as you delve into Oxford's rich history. Start your day at the iconic Oxford Castle and Prison, a historic Norman castle turned prison turned into a visitor attraction. The castle offers guided tours where you'll walk through the ancient crypt and ascend St. George's Tower for panoramic views of the city. The entry fee is approximately $15, and tours usually last around 1.5 hours.

Next, immerse yourself in the scholarly atmosphere of the Bodleian Library. Opt for a guided tour, which costs around $20, to explore the Divinity School, Duke Humfrey's Library, and the Radcliffe Camera. Discover the library's fascinating history, architectural marvels, and its role in various films, including Harry Potter.

Tip: Check the Bodleian Library website for tour availability and book in advance. Tours typically run from 10 AM to 5 PM.

Culinary Delights at Oxford's Finest

Savor the delectable cuisine Oxford has to offer. Start your gastronomic journey at the Old Parsonage Hotel, a charming five-star establishment. The hotel's restaurant, the Parsonage Grill, offers a delightful blend of classic British and European dishes. Indulge in their signature dishes, such as the pan-fried sea bass or the truffle mac 'n' cheese. Prices range from $25 to $40 per dish.

For a taste of Oxford's local produce, head to the Covered Market. Stroll through its historic lanes and stop by The Oxford Cheese Company. Engage your taste buds with a cheese tasting experience for around $15. Learn about the origins and flavors of various cheeses, accompanied by expert recommendations.

Tip: The Old Parsonage Hotel restaurant is open from 7 AM to 10 PM. The Covered Market operates from 8 AM to 5:30 PM.

Punting on the Cherwell River

Experience Oxford from a different perspective with a leisurely punt on the Cherwell River. Cherwell Boathouse, located at Bardwell Road, offers punt hire starting at $25 per hour. Glide along the serene river, passing by lush meadows and picturesque bridges. Pack a picnic and make it a romantic outing or a laid-back family adventure.

If you prefer a guided experience, consider a chauffeured punt tour. The Magdalen Bridge Boathouse provides tours for around $40 per person, offering insightful commentary on Oxford's history and architecture as you float along the river.

Tip: Cherwell Boathouse opens at 10 AM, and last punt hire is usually around 5 PM. Magdalen Bridge Boathouse tours run from 10:30 AM to 4 PM.

Captivating Theatrical Performances

As evening descends, indulge in the arts with a visit to the Oxford Playhouse. Located on Beaumont Street, this historic venue hosts a variety of theatrical performances, from classic plays to avant-garde productions. Ticket prices range from $20 to $50, depending on the show and seating.

Alternatively, explore the New Theatre Oxford for a diverse range of entertainment, including musicals, comedy shows, and live performances. Ticket prices vary but typically start at $30.

Tip: Check the Oxford Playhouse and New Theatre Oxford websites for show schedules and book your tickets in advance. Evening performances usually start around 7:30 PM.

Cherished Strolls Through Oxford's Gardens:

Conclude your day with a leisurely stroll through Oxford's enchanting gardens. The University of Oxford Botanic Garden, founded in 1621, is a haven of tranquility. Admission is around $10, and the garden showcases a diverse collection of plants from around the world. Take a guided tour or explore at your own pace, enjoying the serenity of this green oasis.

For a more secluded experience, head to the Oxford University Parks. Open from dawn to dusk, these expansive parks offer picturesque landscapes, lakes, and vibrant flowerbeds. Pack a picnic, unwind, and relish the peaceful ambiance.

Tip: The University of Oxford Botanic Garden opens at 9 AM and closes at 6:30 PM. Oxford University Parks are accessible throughout the day.

In the heart of Oxford's historical tapestry, your journey becomes a cherished collection of moments. From exploring ancient castles and libraries to savoring culinary delights and gliding on the tranquil Cherwell River, every experience weaves together tradition and innovation.

The Old Parsonage Hotel, with its timeless charm, sets the stage for culinary delights that linger on the palate. The Covered Market, a bustling hub of local flavors, adds a dash of authenticity to your gastronomic escapade. Punting on the Cherwell River offers a serene interlude, allowing you to connect with the city's natural beauty.

As the curtains rise at the Oxford Playhouse and New Theatre, the cultural richness of the city unfolds. Theatrical performances become a gateway to emotions, laughter, and thought-provoking narratives. Oxford's gardens, from the meticulously curated Botanic Garden to the expansive University Parks, provide a tranquil finale to your day.

Craft your Oxford odyssey with meticulous planning, savoring each moment and letting the city's charm guide you. From dawn to dusk, let Oxford's history and innovation intertwine, leaving you with memories that stand the test of time.

Made in the USA
Monee, IL
25 February 2025